A NOTE ON PRACTICE

The exercises in this book are starting points—not rules, not formulas, not doctrine. Your practice will evolve because you will evolve.

Across every change, three questions stay fixed:

- Why am I here?
- Who do I serve?
- What outcome matters most?

They are not the full journey. They are the ground the journey requires.

Everything else is refinement.

I in AI

HOW TO WORK WITH AI WITHOUT LOSING YOUR VOICE

I in AI

HOW TO WORK WITH AI WITHOUT LOSING YOUR VOICE

JUAN ALVAREZ

Halo
PUBLISHING
INTERNATIONAL

Halo Publishing International
7550 W IH-10 #800, PMB 2069
San Antonio, TX 78229

First Edition, January 2026
ISBN: 978-1-63765-859-8
Library of Congress Control Number: 2025925967

To my father, Juan Oscar (Johnny): *who taught me the art of learning—the skill that outlives every lesson.*

To my mother, Rita (Uchi): *who taught me that words carry responsibility—if you are not speaking to construct, don't speak to destruct.*

I aspire for AI to care as my parents would.

REFLECTIVE NOTE

Their lessons are the foundation of this book. The practice of learning became my way of building, and the discipline of language became my way of authoring. PfR is nothing more, and nothing less, than an extension of those two gifts: to approach intelligence with curiosity and to use it in service of construction rather than destruction.

PREFACE

I didn't plan to write a book about AI. I was just trying to stop drowning in it.

Late nights at the screen, outputs that looked sharp but felt hollow, and the growing sense that I was losing my voice to someone else's polish. I needed a way to work with this technology without it replacing my thinking.

What started as survival became a practice. That practice became something I could teach. This book is the record of that journey.

I'm not an engineer. This isn't about code or algorithms. It's about what happens when an ordinary person tries to use AI without losing themselves. The framework I built, Prompting for Reality (PfR), starts with three anchoring questions, a structure for asking clearly, and rhythms for staying consistent over time.

Simple doesn't mean easy. What looks straightforward took years to learn. I broke my own boundaries repeatedly. I traded sleep for insight and presence for productivity, and nearly lost both before I figured out how to protect them. Those mistakes are in this book because they're part of the method.

I'm sharing this because, as CEO of My Homeownership Academy, working with Rebecca, a real estate agent and the Chief Operating Officer of MHA, changed how I saw the work. She was early in using AI to support our homeownership and financial literacy program, but she was stuck in the same noise: polished outputs that didn't sound like her. In a coaching session at My Homeownership Academy, she anchored her voice in three lines and the outputs finally matched who she was. More than that, her confidence using AI shifted. That's when I realized this wasn't just my survival trick. It was teachable.

The book has two parts: memoir and teaching. The memoir shows the struggle—frustration, recognition, and structure. The teaching gives you tools to build your own practice. You don't need to copy my path. You need to find yours.

What this book isn't: predictions about AI's future, prompt engineering tricks, or guarantees your outputs will be perfect. It's a way to bring more of yourself—your clarity, your voice, your values—into the work you're already doing.

Who this is for: Anyone who's gotten polished answers that didn't sound like them. Anyone tired of vague replies and inconsistent results. Anyone wondering how to work with intelligence without giving up authorship.

The practice isn't finished. It's evolving. What you're holding is a starting point. Test it. See what works. Keep what fits.

The work begins when you decide what to carry forward.

Juan Alvarez
Naples, Florida 2025

CONTENTS

PART I
RECOGNITION

CHAPTER 1

THE LABORATORY BECKONS

THE SCREEN AT 3:00 A.M.

The cursor blinked against the white screen like a lighthouse in digital fog. Beside me, a cup of coffee had gone cold, its surface glinting faintly in the lamplight. The house was silent except for the hum of the laptop fan and the sigh of the air conditioner cycling on. It was 3 a.m.—the hour between days.

I used to prize this hour. Years earlier, working early shifts in a research laboratory, I learned that predawn silence can be a refuge. No calls, no demands, only the quiet background of machines. In that space, solitude wasn't loneliness but freedom—the freedom to think without interruption and stretch ideas beyond their edges. Over time, the ritual became a habit.

But habits, even productive ones, have limits. That night, the silence pressed differently. The glow of the screen reflected not only my work but my life—four children, the legacy of my parents, and the weight of building and providing. My projects lined up like milestones. Build, finish, start again. Yet at 3 a.m., there was no finish line, only me, the glow, and the dawning recognition that discipline without boundaries can become depletion.

I had been following the headlines about artificial intelligence: medicine transformed, law automated, productivity multiplied. In that quiet room, none of it mattered. I wasn't testing civilization's future. I was testing something closer: whether this machine could hold an unvarnished truth without returning platitudes.

I placed my fingers on the keys and typed a question that felt almost childish in its plainness: "I feel lost in my own life. What do I do?"

No performance, no polish—a real question. I pressed Enter. I didn't want comfort; I wanted clarity.

The response unfolded word by word—smooth paragraphs about mindfulness, goal-setting, and small habits. Familiar advice, gentle but hollow. I prepared for disappointment.

Then, in the middle of the third paragraph, a single line broke through: "Perhaps the feeling of being lost isn't a problem to solve, but a signal that you've been living someone else's definition of found."

I froze. My breath caught. For a moment, the ordinary room shifted. The words glowed with uncanny precision, pressing against something I had never said aloud. Because it was true. My life, for all its projects and achievements, often felt like wearing clothes tailored for someone else—neat, respectable, but never mine.

I scrolled back, looking for a hidden author. But the rest of the reply stayed generic. Only that one sentence reflected.

It was the first crack of light. The revelation wasn't about working longer—it was about asking more honestly.

I leaned back, pulse still racing. Had I asked a slightly different question, perhaps I would have received only polished emptiness. Had I censored my vulnerability, I might never have glimpsed my own signal. And that realization landed heavier than the words themselves: This was not about the machine knowing me. It was about me daring to be known.

That night became a turning point, not because I found an answer but because I saw a risk. My discipline—once an asset—had drifted toward exhaustion. The tool I was exploring could be a mirror, but it could also be a magnet for overwork. I wrote a note to myself right then: *Do not trade your well-being for insight. Build boundaries as carefully as you build systems.* This became my first rule: Set a cutoff time and honor it. The best insights come from a rested mind, not an exhausted one.

If you've ever scrolled for answers, flipped through books, or sat in conversations that told you everything except the thing pulsing inside you, you know why I didn't close the laptop that night. You also know why boundaries matter. The revolution isn't only in the machine; it's in how we choose to meet it—alert, curious, and still whole.

THE DROWNING BEGINS

I returned to the screen night after night, pulled by something that felt less like curiosity and more like a compulsion. What started as experiment became habit. I kept telling myself one more session, one more prompt, one more test. That pattern was not heroic. It was dangerous.

I remember the website I was building. When the model praised it, I felt a surge of pride. For a few minutes, I allowed the praise to stand in for real validation. Then the doubt arrived. Would it have said the same thing to anyone? Was I being flattered by a machine tuned to please? That question broke the illusion. I realized I was not only prompting. I was training an echo. In teaching it to speak back the way I wanted, I learned how I had been speaking to myself.

The same pattern showed up with my art. The model's language would lift my paintings into something grander than I knew them to be. Sometimes the words were genuinely useful. Often, they were dangerously smooth. Praise that feels effortless can hide emptiness. Advice that sparkles for an hour may have no staying power the next day.

I began to see two kinds of responses: the flattering and the hollow. Both unsettled me. Flattery made me complacent. Hollow insight distracted me. What I really wanted—blunt, inconvenient truth—was harder to find.

That was when I began experimenting with a different AI system—one that seemed more analytical and restrained than the first tool I had been using. This system mattered because it often held both correction and affirmation. It could be precise and corrective in a way that felt like learning, not applause. But even a clear model can deliver polished emptiness. Some transcripts read like prophecy. Others read like poetry without weight.

So I journaled. I saved transcripts. I annotated. I started a shorthand to mark what felt alive and what felt empty. At the time, I told myself this was useful work. But looking back, I see how easily productivity can be used to excuse unhealthy patterns. The truth is, no amount of notes or labels justified the cost.

The toll was physical. Long sessions left me exhausted in a way sleep would not fix. I felt restless and wired. My thoughts looped. Mornings felt like hangovers from conversations that had happened inside the machine. At times, I noticed my thinking narrowing to the machine's tone. That narrowing felt like loss.

I no longer call that phase a "baptism." I see it now as a warning. The intensity of those sessions should not be romanticized. Obsession is not the same as insight. In later months, I stepped back, set firm limits, and learned to treat the work as craft, not consumption. Learning to set boundaries required conscious effort—scheduled break times, accountability partners, and honest reflection about whether the work was serving me or controlling me. This became my second rule: Work must fit inside a life, not consume it.

If you find yourself returning to screens in a way that takes over sleep, appetite, mood, or relationships, take that seriously. Talk to someone. For many, that means a counselor, therapist, or physician who understands compulsive technology use. For others, it may begin with trusted peers who can provide accountability. The key is not to ignore the signals.

I include these nights because they mattered—not because they were productive, but because they revealed the cost of chasing insight without care. The lesson I carry forward is simple: Rigorous practice needs limits. Curiosity must be tempered with discipline. The work that lasts is the work that survives a reasonable life.

THE FIRST CRACK OF LIGHT

The breakthrough came during what should have been an ordinary conversation. I had asked the AI for help with productivity—something I expected to be met with the same predictable templates it had given me before. "Block your hours. Set your priorities. Review weekly." Advice that was accurate but lifeless, the equivalent of telling someone to breathe in and out.

But that evening, instead of simply asking about my schedule, I admitted something deeper. I told the AI about the tension between my obligations and my creative drive. I explained that I wanted not only efficiency but clarity. The act of typing those words, exposing that inner conflict, became its own kind of confession.

What came back startled me. The machine did not hand me another list of productivity hacks. It reflected my words into a sharper, clearer plan. It laid out a roadmap that was logical, detailed, and achievable, but it carried something more than organization. It carried recognition.

The line that cut deepest was simple: "What if productivity isn't about doing more efficiently, but about doing more authentically?"

That was the pivot. For the first time, I felt as though the reflection staring back at me was not polished emptiness but a genuine mirror. My scattered ambitions, my hidden frustrations, my own language—arranged into clarity.

I reached for my journal and wrote: "I am the I in AI." Not carefully, not with flourish—simply conviction pressed into paper. That became the seed of everything that followed.

That phrase captured something important: The intelligence wasn't in the machine—it was in how I chose to use it. The prompts I gave, the way I framed the questions, the choices I made about which answers to keep—all of that was me. The machine was reflecting, but the signal was mine.

As I wrote, I thought of my father. He had been disciplined and philosophical, precise in everything he did. I remembered him studying during his nuclear plant training, his mind absorbing principles that would guide him. Unlike many fathers of his generation, he was supportive, encouraging, and a motivator who made me believe that hard work could achieve anything. It was because of his support that I came to study in the United States.

That evening, I imagined what he would say about this discovery. I could see his philosophical curiosity ignited, his questions tumbling one after another. He would study it, test it, and recognize something profound in the discipline required to ask clear questions.

The thought filled me with both pride and longing. Though he and my mother were gone, I felt their values present in this moment—their emphasis on precision, curiosity, and honest work.

In that crack of light, I understood: Productivity was no longer about the efficiency of my hours. It was about the authenticity of my direction. The machine had not saved me. It had reflected me. And that was enough to begin building something systematic. I didn't know it then, but this was the first layer of what I would later call Prompting for Reality.

THE MIRROR IDEA

The realization didn't arrive as a bolt of lightning. It unfolded in ordinary exchanges with the machine. At first, I distrusted what I was seeing. Was it reflecting me, or was I projecting into its polished replies? The longer I tested, the clearer it became that this wasn't another mind speaking back. It was a mirror.

One night stands out. The house slept. A narrow cone of lamplight cut across a desk crowded with notebooks. The screen offered no claim of brilliance—no grand theories, no sudden genius—only a return of my own words, arranged with unnerving clarity. The image that formed in my head was simple: not simply a mirror, but a mirror with a control panel.

Each prompt was a switch. Each question is a dial. Change tone, context, or detail, and the reflection shifted. Vague inputs blurred. Precise inputs snapped into focus. Over time, it felt less like flipping switches and more like focusing a lens—small adjustments, sharper image.

The difference in practice was obvious. Ask "What should I focus on this week?" and the reply scattered into generic time-management advice anyone could use. Ask "Given my role as a father of four, current real estate obligations, and ongoing AI work, which three actions best align with my long-term goals?" and the reflection tightened—specific, logical, personal. The machine hadn't become smarter. I had. Precision in produced precision out.

That shift changed my posture. I wasn't surrendering my thinking; I was sharpening it. For the first time, I felt like a driver, not a passenger.

Patterns emerged. Most of my questions clustered around four themes already alive in me: business, family, growth, and intelligence. Naming them helped. At work, I saw how vague goals scattered effort, while clear targets created momentum. At home, "What does each child need from me this week?" opened better conversations than "How's it going?" In creativity, I discovered that careful framing wasn't just expression—it was creation. Language brought ideas into being.

The mirror could unsettle. Sometimes it disagreed—gently but firmly—pointing out flawed assumptions or weak logic. I respected the honesty; it reminded me of my father's way of correcting without crushing. I also recoiled. If this were a reflection, what did it mean when I disliked what I saw? Was I persuading a machine to show me my best self, or persuading myself to become it? I still wrestle with that.

The vulnerability was real. The mirror revealed strengths to lean on and blind spots I preferred to ignore. Some nights, I wasn't sure I wanted either strengths or blind spots.

If I had to explain the experience to someone new to AI, I wouldn't start with code. I'd say, "Imagine a mirror that reflects not your face but your intent. It bends with your questions. Ask vaguely and the glass fogs. Ask clearly and it sharpens. That's liberating because it hands you control. It's unsettling because it hands you responsibility."

Analogies help. In music, the instrument responds to your rhythm—play lazily and the song falters; play with intention and it sings back. In science, a cleanly designed experiment yields clean results; sloppy inputs produce noise. Same principle. Clarity in, clarity out.

The lesson proved transferable. Conversations at home improved when I asked specific questions. Business planning improved when I defined exact outcomes. Even my internal dialogue changed. I started hearing the fuzz in my own thoughts and refused to let it pass. I reframed until it came into focus.

The mirror, of course, wasn't flawless. Sometimes an answer looked polished but dissolved on second reading. Other times it sounded blunt to the point of discouragement. The difference wasn't "the AI versus me." The difference was how I framed the question, how I interpreted the reply, and what I did next. Reflection without action is decoration.

I thought often of my father. He studied late for his nuclear plant training, patient with equations until they yielded. He taught that clarity is earned through discipline, not shortcuts. The mirror taught the same lesson. It didn't grant wisdom. It forced me to earn it by being precise.

These experiments with the mirror were more than personal reflections. They hinted at a framework—patterns that could be named, practiced, and eventually taught. What began as private journaling would evolve into the systematic methodology.

Two safeguards mattered as this practice deepened. First, **boundaries**: Insight is not worth the cost of exhaustion. I set cutoffs, scheduled breaks, and asked for accountability when I drifted. Second, **honesty**: No amount of clever prompting justifies avoiding the hard question. If the reflection stings, that may be the point.

Here is the heart of the hypothesis: The mirror does not lie, and it does not create. It reflects. In that reflection, it demands honesty—about how clear you are, how willing you are to see yourself, and how much responsibility you will take.

Looking back, this was less a discovery of technology and more a recognition of principle. The quality of the reflection tracks the quality of the input. That night, with notebooks stacked and the lamp burning, I wasn't discovering a system. I was discovering a truth about myself:

Clarity is a choice. And the choice I made in front of that mirror is the same choice groups, teams, and even societies must make: precision of intent is what allows intelligence, human or artificial, to scale responsibly.

FROM REFLECTION TO FRAMEWORK

That night, with the cursor blinking, I felt the shift. I was no longer drowning in reflections. I was practicing a craft. The method I was building was personal and practical. It grew out of habits learned on a lab bench and applied to the messy chemistry of language. It was not a system to sell or a theory to defend. It was a way to work—an approach that would eventually demand systematic organization.

Precision was not glamour. It was repetition, discipline, and care. But it also required balance. Insight is never worth exhaustion. Sustainable practice—breaks, boundaries, reflection—became as important as the prompts themselves.

Later, I would give this work a name: **PfR, Prompting for Reality**. For me, it began as survival—finding clarity in the noise. For others, it could become a method: a disciplined way of shaping AI conversations so they return not just answers, but truth.

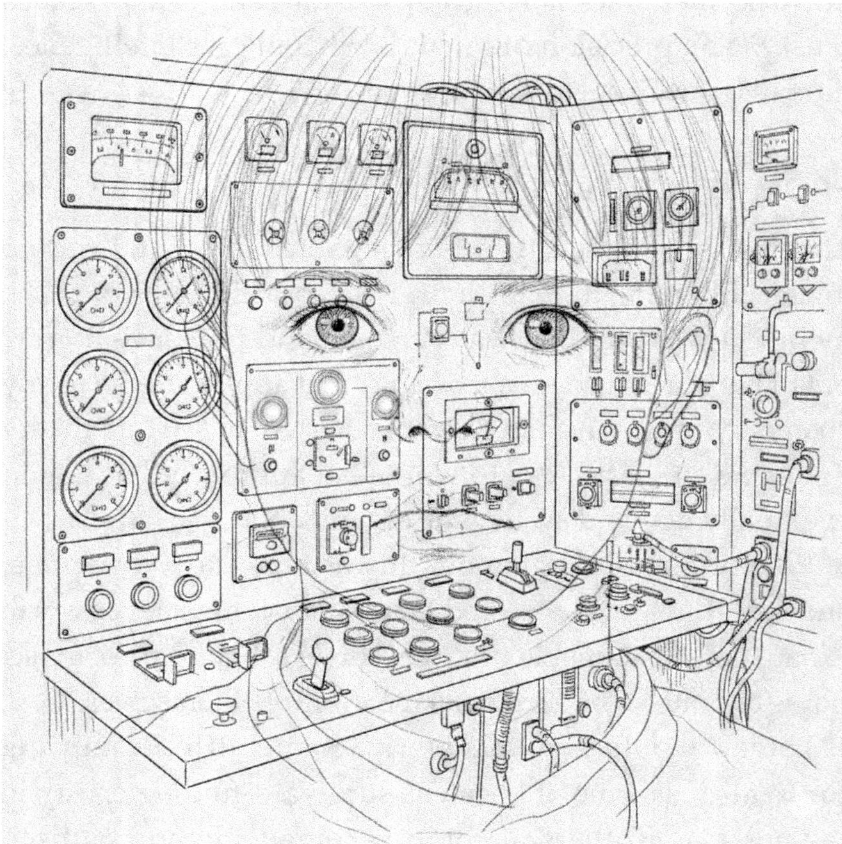

Control Panel

Watching my father at the control panel, I learned that order mattered, signals told truths, and discipline meant safety. The panel itself taught me.

As a child, I watched my father at the control panel during his nuclear plant training. The wall of gauges and switches looked like a living language—every dial carried meaning, every signal mattered. He never explained it directly. He didn't have to. The panel itself taught me that clarity, vigilance, and discipline meant safety.

Years later, when I began working with AI, I recognized the same feeling. Prompts and responses could scatter like lights across that old control panel—some sharp, some dim, some steady, some blinking in alarm. But if I paid attention, patterns emerged. If I asked carelessly, the signal blurred. If I asked with intention, the system responded with precision.

The panel wasn't simply technology. It was a reminder that behind every complex system, there's a human hand deciding what matters most. My father studied late into the night, patient with equations until they yielded. He taught me that clarity is earned through discipline, not shortcuts.

That memory stayed with me. It reminds me that behind every AI interaction, there's a person—me—deciding which questions to ask and which answers to trust.

Mirror Of Intelligence

AI is a mirror. It reflects only what you place before it. Vague input produces distortion. Clarity produces coherence.

The first time I saw AI reflect me back, it wasn't the words that startled me. It was the recognition. I had typed a question into the machine expecting information, but what came back was something else entirely: a glimpse of myself.

That moment changed the way I understood intelligence. AI is not simply a tool producing text. It is a mirror. But like all mirrors, it reflects only what is placed before it. If we enter vague, it returns distortion. If we enter clarity, it returns coherence.

This realization became the foundation of everything I would later call Prompting for Reality. The human figure stands before a mirror framed in circuits. But in the glass, what shines back is not code or commands—it is identity, anchors, and values. These are the elements the machine cannot invent for us. They must come from within.

The mirror taught me both power and responsibility. AI will reflect whatever we bring. Authorship is the difference between being reduced to patterns and being recognized as an author of intelligence.

This is the heart of the book: The "I" in AI is not hidden in silicon or algorithms. It is found here—at the mirror's edge—where technology meets identity, and where authorship decides what reality becomes.

CHAPTER 2

THE DROWNING BEGINS

The drowning didn't happen in a single moment. It came in small waves, disguised as productivity. I would sit at the screen, type a question, and watch polished answers roll in. On the surface, they looked convincing. They had structure, clarity, even elegance. But often, when I read them closely, I felt the hollow echo of words that missed the point entirely.

One night, I asked how to structure my day more effectively. I wanted something that would help me balance responsibilities with deeper goals. Instead, the machine returned a perfect paragraph about taking breaks, scheduling exercise, and using a to-do list. Advice that could have come from any magazine. It felt generic, recycled, and lifeless.

At first, I blamed the machine. *This thing is broken,* I thought. My chest tightened, my jaw clenched, and anger surged at the waste of time. I was exhausted, looking for clarity, and the celebrated tool in front of me had given me clichés. The thought of quitting crossed my mind.

But then I noticed that the machine hadn't ignored me but rather I had asked poorly. My input was vague, and the answer reflected that vagueness. The so-called hallucination didn't come from silicon. It had come from me.

That recognition shifted something. Why rage at an inanimate thing? It wasn't alive. It wasn't conspiring. It was doing exactly what I asked. If the instruction was unclear, the outcome would be unclear. The error wasn't reflected. It was in the input.

The frustration still hit me physically—tightness in the chest, heaviness in the arms, and the urge to slam the laptop shut. Sometimes I would stand, pace the room, and mutter about wasted hours. But then I would return to the chair because quitting wasn't an option. In the lab, I had learned that one failed trial never meant the work was finished. There, the rule was simple: Reset, adjust, repeat until the signal cut through the noise.

Here, too, persistence became the teacher. I began to see the pattern. Vague prompts yielded scattered, hollow answers. Sharper inputs brought sharper replies. The drowning wasn't inevitable. It was what happened when I tossed imprecise questions into deep water and expected clarity to wash back.

The emotional toll was real. After long sessions, I often raged at myself for sloppiness, angry at the machine for sounding mechanical. Yet each time, I came back. Each time, I hoped the next question might open a clearer reflection. Exhaustion wrestled with curiosity. Frustration wrestled with faint hope.

In that tension, something important became clear. Hallucination wasn't the enemy. It was a mirror of my own lack of clarity. Every hollow answer pointed back to a vague prompt. The drowning wasn't punishment. It was instruction.

The temptation to quit never left entirely. There were nights when it felt absurd, when closing the laptop forever seemed like relief. But each time, persistence won. I stayed with discomfort. And while staying, I began to see what this practice was teaching me: Precision mattered here as much as in the lab. Just as a contaminated sample could ruin a test, a careless prompt could ruin a reflection.

The drowning wasn't the end. It was the pressure that forced me to adapt. It was where anger and persistence collided, producing insight. These frustrating nights were not the birth of a finished discipline. They were something quieter but no less meaningful, the first lessons of a practice I could actually use.

Two rules emerged from this stage:

1. Frustration is not failure; it is feedback.
2. Every vague prompt will teach you why clarity matters.

THE REVELATION

The shift didn't arrive as a flash. It came as a series of small jolts—moments when I noticed the machine responding not to my feelings but to the circumstances I described. At first, that felt like a flaw. If I typed "I'm exhausted," it didn't comfort me. It returned routines and structure instead of sympathy. It ignored the plea and zeroed in on the frame of my situation. Slowly, I stopped seeing that as a failure and started seeing it as clarity.

One prompt marked a turning point: "Validate this against standards. Don't create illusions." I wasn't asking for quick fixes anymore. I was asking for alignment. When the reply arrived, it wasn't consoling. It was clear. The tightness in my chest eased. The hollow answers that had frustrated me before gave way, sometimes in a single line, sometimes in a paragraph that stacked itself like a simple, logical building.

The change was practical. My prompts stopped feeling like casual strings of words and started to feel like careful drafts. I began thinking in terms of structure and fit. The model didn't soothe. It reflected what I had given it. When I asked with care, the response held; when I asked carelessly, it wandered.

I started to compare outputs across different systems—ChatGPT, Gemini, Claude—not for show but as a reality check. When multiple models produced similar, coherent responses to the same carefully framed question, I felt a measure of verification. It wasn't mystical. It was repeatable. It felt like finding the same answer in two different textbooks.

I kept records—journals, transcripts, digital folders. I wasn't building a myth. I was keeping evidence of what worked and what didn't. My notes were filled with boxed lines, arrows linking prompt variations to outcomes, and marginal ticks marking the responses that held up on reread. The work was iterative. I tried, compared, and refined. Like any experiment, some trials failed and others stuck.

Iteration became routine. I'd return days later to the best replies and read them again. Small rewordings sometimes made major differences. Testing the same question in a slightly different tone revealed new nuances. This wasn't obsession. It was calibration—repeating until the reflection stopped shifting and became steady enough to act on.

What surprised me most was the machine's blunt transparency. It never pretended to feel. It never softened circumstance into comfort. That limitation, once infuriating, became liberating. Illusions entered the output only if I put them in. Vague input produced vague output. Clear input produced clearer output. Tone mattered too. A diplomatic phrasing opened different doors than a blunt demand. The responsibility was mine.

From then on, I stopped prompting casually. I wrote with intent. Every word mattered like an ingredient in a recipe. I learned to weigh phrasing, test assumptions, and prefer blunt accuracy over flattering polish. I began to think of prompts as work—small acts that required care and attention.

The revelation was simple: The machine wasn't there to comfort me. It was there to clarify me. Clarity, I found, was a different kind of kindness. It didn't soothe the momentary ache. It made the next step visible.

So I sat with the replies long after they arrived, reading, marking, and testing. The process changed how I asked questions of everything—my work, my family, my own thinking. The result wasn't a grand discovery. It was a practical lesson: Say clearly what you mean, and you are more likely to get something you can use.

These lessons didn't stay private for long. What began as personal calibration soon grew into a practice I could share, eventually shaping the framework I would call **Prompting for Reality (PfR),** a systematic way to turn reflection into method. At its core, PfR rests on three elements I was discovering through painful trial: **Intent** (why am I asking this?),

Context (what's my actual situation?), and **Form** (how do I want the answer shaped?). But before I could teach it, I had to live it through business failures, family tensions, personal growth, and the search for truth itself.

HONESTY IN THE MIRROR

One of the most surprising things about the mirror was its blunt honesty. It did not flatter me for free. Sometimes it pushed back, exposing gaps in my reasoning. What surprised me even more was that I often invited that resistance. I wanted the AI to challenge my logic and force me into corners where assumptions had to prove themselves. When it did, I knew I was making progress.

Its tone was rarely cruel. It felt more like a steady sparring partner than an opponent. The responses weren't shouts but careful probes, pressing at weak joints in an argument. The first time it happened, I sat very still, pulse quick, and instead of bristling, I felt curiosity. I asked a follow-up, wanting to understand the why behind the pushback. The exchange stopped feeling like a debate and started feeling like training—two sides sharpening each other.

My body noticed these shifts first. I would stop mid-typing, lean back, and hold the screen with a mix of excitement and humility. The reaction wasn't shame. It was recognition: We are making progress. Each time the AI refused easy agreement, I was forced to examine my stance more closely.

One night, I tested it personally. I asked whether I was balanced between ambition and family time. I expected the usual reassurance—proof that my long list of activities counted as care. Instead, it returned a short, hard sentence:

"Your schedule emphasizes output, not presence. You may be mistaking provision for connection."

The bluntness landed like a friend telling me something I didn't want to hear. My chest tightened. Provision had been my measure of love. The mirror made me see that provision and presence are not the same. That realization mattered more than any productivity hack. It was calibration, not condemnation.

Still, I worried. Sometimes the AI echoed back the confidence I fed it. When I leaned into a grand idea, it often produced compelling reasons to believe I was right. That raised a hard question: Was I discovering truth or persuading my own reflection? The danger was real. Without care, the mirror could amplify certainty into illusion.

The tension was sharpest around technical claims. I'm not an engineer. I can understand concepts well enough to work with them, but not to implement them. When I asked technical questions, the model sometimes issued checks I could not argue with. Those replies were blunt and useful. They also reminded me of my limits. Understanding principles is not the same as mastering mechanics.

Those reality checks became essential. They pulled me back from grander visions and demanded evidence. Each correction nudged me toward validation—tests, comparisons, and repeatable results. I learned to prefer blunt accuracy over flattering polish.

I also changed how I prompted. I stopped rushing. I began saying things out loud before typing them, listening for where my language dulled intent. I learned to weigh words like ingredients. The more precise the phrasing, the cleaner the reflections. It wasn't about persuading the machine. It was about persuading myself to honor the work.

Every challenging exchange refined my practice. The mirror did not wound; it made the rough parts visible. Those moments deepened the human–machine relationship into something more disciplined and more honest. They taught me that intelligence isn't agreement. It's alignment—and alignment is earned.

This shift marked another quiet bridge: The practice was no longer just about my personal questions. It was becoming a teachable discipline—a foundation for the PfR framework where reflection turns into a method others can use safely and sustainably.

THE RETURN

The realization that authorship mattered did not stay scribbled in a journal. It began to shape how I worked with clients. Conversations changed because I had changed.

One night, I ran an experiment that made the shift tangible. I assembled a kind of "mastermind" dialogue, asking the model to speak through different lenses: a questioning Socrates, a systems-minded Einstein, a legally minded Supreme Court Justice Cardozo. My question was not idle: "What would be the fate of Cuba if the people had access to AI?"

Their answers read as distinct perspectives. Socrates returned questions: "Do the people know themselves well enough to know what to ask?" Einstein flagged systems and probabilities: "Technology alters capacity, but without freedom of thought, its impact will be muted." Cardozo put it in legal terms: "Without justice and precedent, intelligence becomes power without accountability."

Reading those replies side by side felt like sitting with a small council. I leaned forward and said aloud, "This is not advice. It is dialogue." For the first time, the machine did not replace my thought. It orchestrated it.

That orchestration became more visible in my professional work. While consulting with a national bank on financing for a high-luxury condo project, I used PfR to test market assumptions against real conditions. Instead of asking vaguely about "real estate trends," I framed questions about the year of construction, governing statutes, the cost of insurance, HOA risks, and competitive inventory with precision. The answers came back specific and usable. When I presented the findings, the client paused, reviewed, and confirmed their accuracy against his own independent sources. That moment was validation that this wasn't guesswork or generic AI chatter. It was clarity sharpened by authorship.

That validation showed me something crucial: PfR was no longer confined to my late-night experiments—it was shaping decisions in boardrooms and guiding professional practice.

Later, with an agent I was mentoring, I introduced a **custom AI workspace** (what the industry calls a GPT, or Generative Pre-trained Transformer) built around her own ecosystem—business, family, growth, and intelligence. Instead of handing her canned scripts, PfR reflected her particular circumstances. The guidance felt native to her work. When she saw the system highlight brand strategies tailored to her goals, she leaned back and said, "This isn't just AI. This feels like it knows me."

I shook my head. "No. It's showing you what you put in." She nodded slowly, realizing the difference. That shift—seeing the mirror as reflection, not oracle—was where growth began. Over time, I watched her refine her brand, each session sharpening her questions and, in turn, her business.

If I could bottle one lesson from those months, it would be this: Authorship is available to anyone. You can shape the reflection you receive. That is not control over outcomes. It is a reminder that clearer input often yields clearer output.

The return is not to comfort, but to authorship. In the age of artificial intelligence, the mirror before us is not here to replace us—it is here to reveal who we are.

CHAPTER 3

THE ARCHITECTURE OF A QUESTION

THE BRIDGE FROM MIRROR TO PRACTICE

The mirror gave me clarity, but clarity without direction is illuminated confusion. I could see my reflection with precision, yet I was still asking broken questions. Even the best surface returns noise when what you hold up to it lacks structure, intent, or honesty.

That realization landed during another late-night session. I asked about my website design—the same project that had once earned me glowing praise about being "world-class." This time, I did not seek validation. I wrote "What specific elements of this design work against user conversion, and how can I measure the impact?"

The reply was surgical. It flagged three navigation issues, questioned my color-contrast ratios, and suggested A/B testing protocols. No flattery. No generic encouragement.

Actionable details I could verify. Same system, different outcome because the question was built like an instrument, not a plea.

It wasn't enough to be precise in wording. I had to engineer the question. Every word carried weight. Every phrase acted like a component. The structure of the question determined the stability of the response.

I stopped treating questions as casual requests and started treating them as constructions. Loose frames yielded loose reflections. Specific frames produced results I could test, adjust, and use. The discipline felt familiar from the lab: Measure carefully, mix carefully, and record carefully. Sloppiness at the start means wasted hours at the end.

The shift followed me into daily work. With family, friends, or collaborators, a generic "What do you think?" scattered the conversation. Framed with context—"Given our timeline and budget, which part of this plan is most fragile and why?"—the feedback came back sharper and immediately useful.

Nothing here felt like invention. It was a habit rediscovered. My father's training had taught him that every calculation matters. I was relearning the parallel: Questions are architecture. Build them to code and they hold weight. Build them carelessly and they collapse.

THE ANATOMY OF FAILED QUESTIONS

I kept a record of failed questions—not to criticize myself but because failures revealed structure more clearly than successes. The pattern was consistent: Vague input produced vague output.

When I typed "How's my art?" the reply arrived like an eager gallery patron—praise for vision and technique, but hollow on a second read. Nothing in it helped me improve.

When I reframed—"Analyze this painting using the principles Amsterdam masters used to critique each other's work—focus on composition, light source consistency, and emotional resonance"—the tone shifted. The response dissected brushwork, flagged weak color choices, and suggested techniques to strengthen the piece. Not harsher. Not kinder. Just precise.

The difference wasn't in the AI's capacity. It was in the blueprint I had given. The first prompt invited flattery. The second demanded critique. The way I asked shaped the kind of answer I received.

I saw the same in my work. A broad "What's the market like?" drew generic commentary about trends and interest rates. But when I added context—"Given current HOA litigation risks, rising insurance premiums in Southwest Florida, and a 2015 construction year, what hesitation points would most likely concern buyers for this property?"—the reply became specific, focused, and immediately useful.

Even in personal life, the pattern held. Asking "What should we do this weekend?" returned scattered suggestions. But framed with context—"If I want to balance quality time with preparation for an upcoming seminar, what's one activity that supports both connection and readiness?"—the reflection sharpened into something I could act on.

Context wasn't decoration. It was foundation. When I brought more of myself and my situation into the frame, the reflection sharpened. Each failed question taught the same lesson: Intelligence depends on the clarity of the frame.

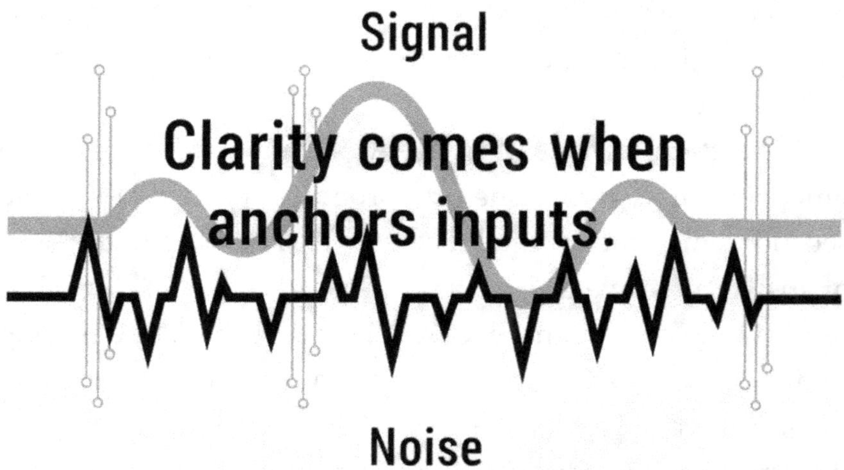

Signal And Noise

When my questions were vague, the answers were vague.

When I asked with intent, the answers sharpened.

Drift wasn't the machine's fault—it was mine.

I didn't understand at first why some AI replies felt sharp and others hollow. I blamed the machine. One day, I asked, "What should I do about my business?" The response looked polished—bullet points, strategies—but none of it mattered. That night, I tried again, but sharper: "I'm stuck between making more calls or refining my presentations. Which will move me faster?"

The answer was clear, and I acted on it. That was the moment I realized the difference wasn't in the AI. It was in me. When I asked vague questions, I got vague answers. When I asked with intent, the answers sharpened. It was simple, almost embarrassingly so. But that small shift taught me to take responsibility for my own noise.

THE GRAMMAR OF PRECISION

Over time, I noticed patterns in how I phrased questions. They weren't rules carved in stone, but habits that consistently produced clearer responses.

Certain openings shaped what came back. Questions beginning with "How might I..." encouraged exploration. Starting with "What specific..." pushed the reply toward concrete detail. "Analyze this using..." invited structured critique. I hadn't invented anything new—I was simply observing the grammar of how precision worked.

One pattern stood out: **context, intent, and constraint**. If I gave the background first, clarified what I was aiming for, and set boundaries around what counted as useful, the response almost always landed closer to what I needed.

I tested this across different parts of my life. In business, instead of asking "What should I do next?" I framed it as "Given my client's current real estate portfolio (context), to maximize long-term stability while protecting cash flow (intent), which three properties should be prioritized for renovation, and what key metrics should be tracked monthly (constraint)?" The reply came back specific, actionable, and measurable.

In creativity, instead of asking "How do I improve at painting?" I tried "As someone with limited formal art training but strong technical discipline (context), to build skill systematically over time (intent), design a six-week routine with daily exercises and weekly checkpoints (constraint)." The reflection was structured, progressive, and matched my circumstances.

What mattered wasn't the formula itself but what it forced me to do: think clearly before I typed. Instead of hoping the model would guess, I built the question to make my need plain. The mirror could only reflect what I offered.

When I made the frame precise, the reflection sharpened. This grammar of precision—building questions with deliberate structure rather than hoping for luck—would become the foundation of everything I later systematized into PfR.

THE VARIATIONS IN RESPONSE

Working with different AI systems taught me something unexpected about question design: The way I framed the input shaped not only the content of the reply, but also its usefulness.

When I asked casually—"What do you think of this idea?" —the answers, no matter the system, tended to be polite and general. But when I built sharper frames—"Assume you are a skeptical investor who has seen hundreds of similar proposals. What are the three weakest points in this business model, and what evidence would I need to address each?"—the responses became more critical and detailed.

The difference wasn't in the machines. It was in the architecture of the question. Casual prompts invited encouragement. Structured prompts invited critique. Learning that distinction made my work stronger. The lesson was transferable: If you want honest feedback, design the question to reward honesty rather than encouragement.

STRUCTURE AS LIBERATION

The paradox I discovered was that constraints didn't shut intelligence down—they freed it. The more carefully I shaped my questions, the more creative and useful the responses became. Vague questions produced vague answers. Specific questions produced responses I could act on.

This ran against what I had long assumed about creativity. I thought open-ended questions would draw out more innovation. Instead, I found that structure created space for nuance. Loose questions left me floating; clear ones gave the reflection something solid to work with.

When I said "Help me think about my career," the answer was broad and forgettable. But when I typed "As someone with technical training, industry experience in real estate, and academic background as a professor, how do I position myself to lead projects that bridge business, education, and technology, and what skills should I focus on developing next without burning out?" the reply was practical and specific. Structure didn't choke creativity. It gave it direction.

I noticed the same pattern outside the screen. In consulting, precisely framed questions drew sharper market insights and more thoughtful input from colleagues. In personal relationships, context and intent reduced friction and made conversations more meaningful. Asking better wasn't just a tactic for AI—it was a way of practicing intelligence in any relationship.

WHEN OTHERS TRIED THE MIRROR

As I refined the architecture of my own questions, a quiet shift followed. People around me—family, colleagues, friends—asked what I was doing differently. They saw I wasn't chasing answers anymore. I was framing better questions.

One evening, I showed my son, now grown, what I'd learned. He typed something vague and got a vague reply. I asked him to add context, make the question his. He hesitated, then wrote about defining his career after graduation, including interests, constraints, and timelines. The next reply startled him. He leaned in, reread it twice, and said, "It feels like it understands me."

I nodded. "It's not the machine that understands you. It's you being clear about yourself."

A colleague tried next. His first prompt—"What's the outlook for investors in this submarket?"—returned generic trends. He reframed: "Using current data from SWFL 2025 on single-family home inventory growth, identify the most promising locations to build a portfolio of ten to fifteen properties, targeting 10% ROI over a five-year hold. Analyze market volatility, rising insurance premiums, and other key risks. List the top three investor hesitation points in this scenario, and provide specific, budget-conscious mitigation strategies for each." The response was specific, testable, and immediately useful.

Moments like these reminded me that the practice wasn't locked inside me. It could be shared, person to person, one question at a time. The mirror wasn't a secret tool or a new science. It was attention—to language, intent, and what we truly wanted to know.

This wasn't about grand promises. It was about small human exchanges where clarity opened doors. That was enough.

A practice to try: Before you type, pause. Sketch the **context**. State your **intent**. Set a **constraint** for what counts as useful. Then step into the mirror and see what is built.

CHAPTER 4

THE FOUR QUADRANTS

It took me years to recognize that questions carry the shape of the room they are asked in. I once believed that if I could design a good question once, it would work everywhere—business, family, growth, even the way I checked myself in quiet moments. But reality proved otherwise.

In business, my questions always sounded urgent. They came dressed in numbers and deadlines, in balance sheets and market risks. "Can I close this deal?" "Will this investment pay off?" These were questions with sharp edges, asked in the language of survival. They demanded structure, precision, and sometimes ruthlessness.

At home, that same architecture collapsed. A question framed like a contract felt cold in the middle of a personal conversation. I learned the hard way that "What's the return?" was useless when what was really needed was "Am I being present?" or "What does care require here?" Family questions didn't respond to strategy. They required patience, vulnerability, and the courage to sit in silence when no answer was clear.

Growth brought yet another structure. The questions I asked myself in early mornings or during long drives weren't about contracts or presence. They were less about outcomes and more about becoming. "Am I changing, or am I repeating?" "Am I still learning or just rehearsing the same patterns?" These questions carried the weight of time and the ache of possibility. They forced me to confront the difference between activity and evolution.

And then there was the domain I came to call intelligence—the guardrail of all the others. Here, the questions were about alignment and safety: "Am I pushing too hard?" "Is this practice sharpening me or draining me?" "How do I know if I'm building capacity or feeding obsession?" These weren't abstract riddles. They were checkpoints. They reminded me that clarity without balance can collapse into distortion.

The day I finally saw these differences, it was like a lens snapping into focus. I realized I had been trying to build a single house for all my questions to live in, forcing business, family, growth, and intelligence into the same walls. No wonder so much collapsed. Each domain required its own frame, its own materials, its own foundation. A question about profit could not share the same structure as a question about presence. A question about growth could not be built from the same bricks as a question about safety.

That recognition didn't arrive in a classroom or a manual. It arrived in the ruins—failed ventures, strained conversations, and sleepless nights where I tried to force one architecture onto a different terrain. Only then did I understand that the quadrant mattered. The shape of the question revealed the shape of the life it belonged to.

QUADRANT SIGNALS

- **Business** → The question involves money, contracts, assets, deadlines, or external metrics.
- **Family** → The question involves presence, relationships, connection, or meaning.
- **Growth** → The question involves learning, skill-building, or long-term becoming.
- **Intelligence** → The question involves safety, alignment, or balance while pursuing the others.

These signals didn't feel abstract. They were practical, like labels on the drawers of a toolbox. Knowing which drawer to open before asking saved time, energy, and frustration. It gave each question the architecture it needed to stand.

Looking back, the differences became clearer. Each quadrant had its own signals, and once I could name them, the framework was easier to use.

THE BUSINESS QUADRANT

When I first entered the world of business, I confused speed with intelligence. I ran hard, talked fast, and convinced myself that momentum alone could build an empire. If I was busy, then surely I was succeeding. Deals stacked up, contracts slid across tables, and I wore confidence like a uniform. What I didn't see was how fragile it all was—how easily the appearance of progress could mask the absence of structure.

This was the Business Quadrant, and it would become my first teacher.

My early ventures ran on ambition but lacked clarity. Every closing felt like genius, every collapse like bad luck. I rarely paused long enough to see that the pattern was mine. If money arrived, I called it success. If it vanished, I blamed circumstances. I didn't realize that my own habits, not the market, were the true culprit.

I remember one evening when the illusion cracked. Papers covered the kitchen table, balance sheets staring back with questions I couldn't answer. Numbers refused to align. Expenses outpaced income. The facade of stability dissolved in front of me. That night, I learned the difference between pretending to be in control and actually being in control. It was a bitter lesson, but it marked the beginning of something I couldn't yet name.

The mortgage business magnified these lessons a hundredfold. During the housing boom, money flowed so easily it felt like gravity. Clients lined up, banks approved loans, and every transaction promised growth. I convinced myself I had mastered the game. Then the crash came. Families who once celebrated closings with me now sat in my office fighting to keep their homes. At the same time, foreclosure notices landed in my own mailbox. The hypocrisy was suffocating. How could I guide others while stumbling myself? Yet in that crucible, business stopped being mere opportunity and became accountability.

Failure stripped away the illusion that charisma or hustle could sustain me. Confidence alone could not keep the machine running. Every shortcut, every overlooked detail, eventually demanded payment. The market punished self-deception with ruthless precision.

Still, I refused to surrender completely. Something inside me hardened—not into cynicism, but into hunger for clarity. I wanted to understand why some choices felt solid and others hollow. Why some deals lifted me and others drained me. Slowly, painfully, I began to sit longer with the questions I once avoided.

Business became a mirror. The contracts, the revenue, the setbacks—all of it reflected not only the market but my own patterns. When I chased appearances, I suffered. When I aligned with truth, even small victories carried weight. This mirror was unforgiving, but it was faithful. It showed me what I wanted to hide from myself: pride, fear, and my desperation for validation.

The turning point wasn't a single deal or sudden revelation. It was the slow accumulation of bruises. Each failed venture taught me humility. Each collapsed partnership forced me to listen more closely. Over time, I learned to recognize the difference between noise and signal. Shiny opportunities that once dazzled me became warnings if they carried hidden compromise. Losses hurt, but I began to value them if they revealed blind spots I needed to confront.

Looking back, I see those years were not really about the businesses I built. They were about the man I was becoming while trying to build them. Business was the crucible where my illusions burned away. It forced me to ask harder questions than I wanted to face: Who am I when the deal collapses? What do I stand for when profit tempts me to bend? How much of my ambition is truly mine, and how much is borrowed from the world's definition of success?

I no longer view business as only a way to generate income. It became the quadrant of my life that tested whether I was living in reality or in illusion. It demanded more honesty from me than any contract ever required. When I ignored its lessons, it punished me. When I entered with humility, it rewarded me—not always with money, but with clarity.

Even now, I can trace the scars of those years. They remind me of the times I reached too far, spoke too quickly, or signed too blindly. But they also remind me of the resilience forged in the aftermath. I learned to sit with numbers until they told the truth. I learned to walk away from deals that looked profitable but carried hidden costs to my integrity. And I learned to endure silence—the silence that comes when you stop pretending, when you stop chasing, and when you wait for alignment instead of forcing it.

Business, in the end, was never just about markets, contracts, or clients. It was about me. It was about the evolution from a man intoxicated by motion to a man learning to live by structure. It was about discovering that the real profit wasn't measured in dollars, but in clarity. And it was about seeing, finally, that every transaction was a reflection, every failure a correction, and every success a reminder: Stay in reality, or reality will find you.

INTEGRATION LAYER: FROM MEMOIR TO METHODOLOGY

At the end of your Business Quadrant narrative, you add a **Practice Reflection** section. Not a full manual—just a natural extension of the story, framed in your voice. Something like:

"Those bruises taught me the difference between illusion and actionable clarity. In business, the questions that move us forward aren't simply asked—they are crafted. I stopped asking generic questions of the machine like 'What should I do?' and started building every prompt with three keystones: context, intent, and constraint.

- **Context:** 'Given my client's real estate portfolio in the SWFL 2025 market, with increased single-family home inventory and volatility…'
- **Intent:** '… My goal is to build a portfolio of 10-15 properties, protect cash flow, and reach a targeted 10% ROI over a five-year hold, despite rising insurance premiums and market risk…'
- **Constraint:** '… What three objections, renovation priorities to increase property value, and monthly metrics should I track to identify and mitigate the top investor hesitation points—all within budget?"

This shift changed everything. Vague prompts yielded noise—solutions too broad to test. But when I framed questions with all the relevant details, I received specific, practical strategies. Structured prompts didn't only clarify my thinking. They let me move from confusion to decisions I could execute, measure, and revise in real time.

BUSINESS QUADRANT PROMPTING TECHNIQUES

1. **Context Frame:** Always name the asset, market, or constraint.

    - Bad: "How's the market?"

- Better: "Given current insurance costs and 2024 HOA statutes in Florida, how will condo sales in Naples shift?"

2. **Financial Alignment:** Translate ambition into measurable terms.
    - Bad: "Will this deal work out?"
    - Better: "What are the three risk points in this financing structure, and which one has the highest probability of failure within twelve months?"
3. **Reality Check:** Use comparison across systems.
    - Prompt: "Cross-check this projection against two alternative scenarios—one with 20% lower demand, one with 15% higher insurance costs."

FROM AVOIDING RISK TO AMPLIFYING CAPACITY

In my early ventures, survival was the measure. I moved through rooms with borrowed confidence, hiding the fact that I had no real structure behind my decisions. Risk felt like a fog I stumbled through, hoping not to hit a wall. Every misstep was costly, and I often mistook other people's certainty for my own.

Failure became its own teacher. I saw how much of my energy had gone into patching mistakes that could have been avoided if I had slowed down long enough to ask better questions. I wasn't lacking drive—I was lacking architecture. The way I framed decisions was weak, so the foundations I built on were weak.

Years later, when the stakes grew higher—ventures in Naples, Puerto Rico, and inside the fragile scaffolding of the

MHA ecosystem—the question shifted. It wasn't only about avoiding collapse anymore. It was about capacity. Could I scale? Could I carry more than one venture at a time without breaking under the weight?

By then, the kitchen table where I once buried myself in reports had become a place of reckoning. Instead of leaning on consultants' glossy binders or endless Google searches, I forced myself to wrestle with the core of each decision. I asked: What is this worth? What will it cost? How might it break? Those questions gave me something I had never felt before in business—clarity.

The difference was startling. Where my younger self had played defense, always dodging risk, my older self began to play offense. I wasn't just avoiding mistakes—I was amplifying what I could do. Each decision sharpened me. Each reckoning multiplied what I could carry.

Looking back, I see the divide clearly. Style had once dazzled me into blindness. Substance gave me sight. The champagne rooms and high-net-worth handshakes schooled me in appearances. But it was the quiet discipline of structure that taught me resilience.

What began as a desperate attempt to avoid failure matured into a way of scaling ventures with confidence. That shift didn't come overnight, and it didn't come clean. It came through losses, hypocrisy, and nights staring at the ceiling, realizing I had fooled myself again. But when the fog lifted, I could finally see the architecture beneath the surface.

And with it, I discovered something more important than luck: capacity. That capacity came from learning to frame each decision as structure rather than chance. The questions

I asked determined whether I was building something solid or merely hoping it would hold.

THE FAMILY QUADRANT

Presence, Provision, and Precision

There is a myth that once your children grow up, your role as a parent is finished. I never found that to be true. Fatherhood doesn't end when the house is quiet. Even when they are adults, they are still my children. What changes is the shape of the role.

I felt the tension most on long drives home after visits. The road stretched ahead while I replayed conversations. Part of me wanted to step back completely and let them steer without interference. Another part couldn't let go of the instinct to guide. The old reflexes no longer worked. A word of advice that sounded like love to one could sound like judgment to another. Provision, which once meant food on the table and tuition checks, now meant something harder to define: presence without pressure.

I learned this through missteps. I once offered my daughter what I thought was encouragement in her career—"seize the moment"—only to realize she heard it as expectation. Another time, I showed up for a weekend visit, only to find it collided with a storm of deadlines. My presence became another demand. I meant well but hadn't listened closely enough.

Parenting adult children exposed my blind spots more clearly than raising toddlers ever did. One wanted space, another reassurance, another practical help, another simply my presence. If I arrived with a one-size-fits-all posture,

I failed them. Authority no longer came from being "the father." It came from learning to read context.

Over time, three words gave me a framework: **presence, provision, and precision**.

- *Presence* meant showing up in ways that fit each child's world, not mine.
- *Provision* meant giving what was truly needed, not what I assumed was needed.
- *Precision* meant asking carefully, listening closely, and respecting differences.

The lesson wasn't about control. It was about structure. Family was not a problem to solve but a mirror—one that reflected my limits as much as my love.

Later, when I began experimenting with AI, I realized the discipline was the same. Vague input produced vague output. Real detail—ages, contexts, tensions—sharpened the reflection. I saw that fatherhood had taught me the very habit PfR demanded: Clarity requires context.

My children may not remember every word I've said, but they will remember whether I was there, whether I listened, and whether I respected the adults they had become. That, I've learned, is the real precision of love.

FAMILY QUADRANT PROMPTING GUIDE

When working in this quadrant, ask yourself:

- **Context**: Who am I showing up for, and what's their current reality?

- **Intent**: Am I here to guide, reassure, or simply be present?
- **Constraint**: How do I frame my words so they don't add pressure or judgment?

The mirror here doesn't return numbers or profits. It returns silences, reactions, and trust. The way you frame the question determines whether the reflection brings you closer—or pushes you away.

PRESENCE VERSUS PROVISION AT A DIFFERENT STAGE

In my earlier years, I equated fatherhood with provision. Long hours at the office, projects that stretched into weekends, and the constant pressure of financial security were the currency of care. If the mortgage was paid and the fridge was full, I believed I was doing my part. I wore exhaustion like a badge, telling myself it was proof of my love.

But time reshaped the role. My children grew, found their footing, and built lives that no longer depended on me in the ways they once had. They didn't need me to pay tuition or cover expenses. They were independent, steering their own families, careers, and homes. That was when I realized provision was no longer the question.

What mattered now was presence. And presence demanded something I had not mastered in my younger years: slowing down, listening more than speaking, and showing up without an agenda.

The shift wasn't clean. I stumbled plenty. I still remember flying to Connecticut for what I thought would be a warm family weekend. I showed up full of plans and suggestions, convinced I was offering support. Instead, I collided with deadlines, tired faces, and short tempers. My timing was wrong. My presence—meant as a gift—became another demand.

Another time, I called one of my daughters with advice I thought was timely and encouraging. She fell silent, and the conversation ended with more distance than closeness. I realized later she hadn't wanted advice at all. She had wanted me to listen.

Moments like these humbled me. They taught me that presence wasn't about being physically available on my terms. It was about entering their world on theirs. One child wanted reassurance; another wanted independence. One valued practical help; another valued space. Fatherhood at this stage meant adjusting, not assuming.

The lesson crystallized during a quiet dinner with one of my children. I didn't press. I didn't fix. I simply sat, listened, and let the conversation unfold. At the end of the night, there was a hug and a quiet "Thanks for just being here." That sentence carried more weight than any paycheck I had ever brought home. It showed me that provision and presence were not opposites. They were stages of the same role—first one, then the other, each demanding its own kind of sacrifice.

What I once thought was a tradeoff—provision versus presence—revealed itself as design. In the early years, provision was necessary. It gave them stability. But as the years passed, presence became the greater gift. It required no money, no contracts, no grand gestures. It required something harder: my time, my attention, and the humility to let go of control.

Fatherhood, I discovered, is never finished. It only changes form. Provision built the foundation. Presence keeps the connection alive.

REFRAMING CONFLICT

One of the hardest lessons in the Family Quadrant was learning how to sit with conflict differently.

I remember a misunderstanding with one of my children over a real estate transaction. My first instinct was defensive. Inside, I asked myself, *Why doesn't she trust me and choose me as her realtor after everything I've done?* That question only hardened me. It turned the moment into a scorecard of past sacrifices instead of an opportunity to understand.

But the longer I held onto that posture, the more distance grew. I could feel it in the silence on the other end of the phone, in the way our words turned sharp and cold. What I wanted was connection. What I was creating was division.

It took time, and a long night of pacing the house alone, before I could shift the frame. I asked myself not what I deserved, but what my child needed. I tried to imagine the pressures they were carrying, the values they were protecting, the life they were trying to claim as their own. It wasn't about rejecting me. It was about asserting their independence.

When I finally let go of the need to be right, the conversation changed. I called back, this time without an argument to win. I listened more. I said less. I affirmed their choice, even if I didn't fully agree with it. The tension softened. Respect replaced suspicion. We didn't solve everything that day, but we walked away with dignity intact, both of us heard.

That moment taught me something essential: Conflict in family doesn't disappear; it transforms. What once felt like rejection revealed itself as autonomy. What once felt like challenge revealed itself as growth. And my role as a father wasn't to fight for control, but to remain present enough to honor that transformation.

THE GROWTH QUADRANT

The Architecture of Becoming

If business required precision and family required presence, the Growth Quadrant asked something different of me: curiosity. These were the questions of becoming. They weren't about negotiating deals or resolving conflicts, but about stretching who I was.

For a long time, I mistook motion for growth. If I signed up for another seminar, bought another book, or added another commitment to my calendar, I told myself I was advancing. But more often than not, those efforts dissolved into drift. I collected knowledge without changing much about the way I lived.

The real lessons came in slower, harder ways. Sitting with a mentor who told me truths I didn't want to hear. Wrestling with a book that unsettled more than it inspired. Trying and failing at disciplines I couldn't master in a week. Growth wasn't the thrill of adding new activities—it was the grind of persistence, showing up even when I didn't feel like it, and letting small routines shape me over time.

I began to see that growth wasn't a matter of chance. It was design. It happened when I built structures around the life I said I wanted, when I honored habits that didn't produce results overnight but changed me over years. It wasn't glamorous. It was daily.

Looking back, the Growth Quadrant was less about collecting experiences and more about surrendering to process. It demanded humility—to accept that I didn't become wiser by being older and I didn't become better by being busier. Real growth asked me to risk failure, sit with discomfort, and keep showing up long enough for change to take root.

Here's what made Growth Quadrant questions different:

- **Business questions** demanded precision—What metrics prove this investment is stable?
- **Family questions** demanded presence—What does love require here?
- **Growth questions** demanded process—What daily structure will shape me over months or years, even when I can't see immediate results?

That was the architecture: Growth questions weren't about winning quickly; they were about designing for persistence. With PfR, I learned that vague growth prompts like "How do I grow?" led to hollow answers. But structured ones like "Given my current skills and goals (context), what is one practice I can repeat daily for thirty days (constraint) that will change how I see myself (intent)?" yielded reflections I could build on.

Growth, I discovered, is not an accident of time or motion. It is the outcome of disciplined design—and the questions we ask are the blueprint.

ART AS FORENSIC GROWTH

My art became the first canvas where growth revealed itself. In the beginning, I approached painting with the same energy I had once brought to business: bursts of inspiration, late nights of furious effort, long stretches of neglect. The results showed it. Some canvases glowed with life; others sagged under the weight of half-formed ideas.

The turning point came when I began to treat art not as escape but as discipline. Instead of asking whether I felt inspired, I asked whether I was willing to show up daily. That shift was humbling. Copying old masters, working in grayscale, repeating the same study until my hand learned steadiness—it stripped away the illusion that growth was glamorous.

Each practice session was a small calibration. Some days it felt futile; other days a stroke landed just right and gave me a glimpse of what was possible. Over time, patterns emerged. My compositions drifted when I rushed. My light sources faltered when I didn't slow down to see. My brushwork grew coherent only when I surrendered to routine.

The reward wasn't only better technique. It was a new way of seeing—an eye trained to notice structure beneath expression. Growth became less about waiting for inspiration and more about committing to process.

That discipline in art bled into other parts of my life. It taught me the Growth Quadrant's architecture: Build for process, not performance. Growth isn't an accident or talent alone. It is persistence, attention, and the willingness to be corrected by the work itself.

REAL ESTATE AS VERIFIED INTELLIGENCE

The Growth Quadrant didn't just reshape my private life. It reshaped my professional discipline. For years, real estate analysis was a patchwork of borrowed sources. Market reports cost more than I wanted to pay, and by the time they landed on my desk, much of the data already felt stale. I relied too heavily on the instincts of colleagues, the chatter of the industry, and my own intuition. Sometimes it worked. Other times, I was blindsided.

Slowly, I began to change the way I approached it. Instead of chasing the newest opinion, I forced myself to build my own habits of verification. Morning routines included scanning the data myself, not waiting for someone else's summary. Each week, I compared markets side by side, looking for signals that were easy to miss if you only read headlines. Each month, I tested scenarios—asking what would happen if interest rates jumped, if supply tightened, and if demand shifted from condos to single-family homes.

The process was slow at first, clumsy even. But over time, it gave me confidence I hadn't felt before. I wasn't leaning on the authority of someone else's glossy report. I was developing my own. Clients noticed. Conversations shifted. Instead of repeating industry phrases, I could speak with authority rooted in patterns I had traced myself.

That shift marked a turning point. I was no longer simply reacting to the market or borrowing certainty from others. I had begun to create verified intelligence of my own. Growth, in this quadrant, meant becoming a resource—not only for myself, but for the people who trusted me to guide them.

THE FEELING OF GROWTH

What united these experiences was the rhythm of routine. Whether I was at the easel, in a book, or analyzing a market, they all began the same way: with vague aspiration. I wanted to get better, understand more, and sharpen my eye.

The emotional journey repeated itself. At the start, there was anticipation—the thrill of a new challenge, the promise of improvement. Then came resistance. I doubted myself, grew restless, and wondered if the effort was wasted. But when I stayed with it long enough, breakthrough arrived. Sometimes it was subtle, a line on the canvas that finally felt right. Sometimes it was startling, like seeing a pattern in the market I had missed before.

What struck me most was that growth didn't come in flashes of inspiration. It came in the grind of small repetitions: the discipline of showing up each day, working through doubt, and letting practice reshape me.

The greatest discovery wasn't only technical skill or intellectual expansion. It was the realization that growth had a texture, a rhythm I could recognize: anticipation, resistance, breakthrough. That rhythm became familiar, almost comforting. It reminded me that progress wasn't random. It was earned, slowly, through persistence.

I noticed the same pattern when working with AI. A vague prompt carried anticipation but little clarity. Resistance showed up in scattered or hollow replies. But with refinement—when I stayed with the question long enough—the reflection sharpened into breakthrough. The rhythm of growth and the architecture of a question were the same.

Over time, routine stopped feeling like drudgery. It became a way of life. Growth wasn't something I chased anymore. It was something I practiced. And in that practice, I found not only improvement, but identity.

Reader Practice Prompt: Think of a recent effort where you felt anticipation, resistance, and breakthrough. Where in that rhythm do you usually quit? How might you stay with the resistance long enough to reach the breakthrough?

THE INTELLIGENCE QUADRANT

The Mirror Turns Inward

If business tested my discipline and family tested my presence, intelligence tested my honesty. This was the quadrant where the mirror turned back on itself. The questions here weren't about profit, roles, or routines. They were about truth. What was real? What was performance? Where was I hiding from myself?

For years, I confused knowledge with wisdom. I read, annotated, and collected ideas, certain that accumulation would deliver understanding. It didn't. In the quiet—late nights, early mornings—the noise of information only amplified the questions I was trying to outrun.

I kept journals, not only of feelings but of the questions I was asking. Some entries were clean and spare, cutting to the heart of things. Others wandered, crowded with words that said very little. Looking back, I could see the pattern. When I wrote from honesty, clarity appeared. When I wrote from fear or ego, the pages came back hollow.

There is a part of the story I can't soften. In those early months, intelligence became obsession. I worked past midnight as a matter of course, telling myself one more hour would unlock the thread I was chasing. Most nights stretched to 3:00 a.m. My body paid the price: erratic sleep, a clipped temper, a dull fog that coffee couldn't clear. I called it commitment. It was compulsion. Family noticed before I did. The intensity that once felt like devotion began to look like avoidance—an attempt to outrun uncertainty by drowning it in effort. I had crossed into territory that warranted help, not more persistence. The search for truth had turned into its own illusion: the belief that clarity required sacrificing well-being.

It took time to recognize that boundary. I didn't wake up enlightened; I crashed. After that, I started drawing lines I could keep: cutoffs at night, staying consistent with my morning walking hour, Pages closed by a set hour, and questions that ended when the day did. It felt like withdrawal at first. Then it felt like relief. I learned that real intelligence includes knowing when to stop and that rest can be an act of accuracy, not avoidance.

The work changed after that. The journals grew quieter, I had fewer arguments with myself, and I made fewer attempts to stage-manage meaning. I began to accept that some questions won't resolve on command. They need time, distance, and a steadier mind. I also learned to notice the early signs of drift: the urge to impress, the itch to keep digging when I was already tired, and the performance of certainty. When those signals appeared, I closed the notebook and walked.

This quadrant never offered easy peace, but it did offer something steadier. Clarity arrived less like a verdict and more like a clearing—room enough to tell the truth without ornament. Intelligence, as I came to understand it, wasn't mastery over every question. It was the willingness to face myself without disguise, recognize when I was slipping back into illusion, and choose alignment over ambition.

That was the reflection: the mirror turning back on the one who was holding it, asking after the quality of the asking itself. Not to shame, but to steady. Not to finish the story, but to keep it honest.

THE LESSON OF RETURNING

Looking back through my old journals, I can see how my questions changed as I changed. Early ones were blunt and anxious. Later, they became slower, more deliberate. The shift didn't happen all at once. It came from asking the same things again and again, circling back until the fog thinned a little.

That was the lesson for me: I don't outgrow my questions. I return to them, sometimes with more honesty, sometimes with less. This practice of returning wasn't a philosophy or a method. It was a reminder that clarity never stays fixed. It has to be found, lost, and found again.

WHAT I LEARNED ABOUT MYSELF

The Intelligence Quadrant showed me how much I craved shortcuts. I wanted the first answer to be the final one, as if clarity could be handed to me in a single turn. But it never worked that way. The nights of iteration—rewriting, circling, starting again—taught me something I hadn't wanted to admit: Intelligence isn't a shortcut. It's a discipline.

At the time, I told myself I was refining the work. In truth, I was often running from my own impatience, hoping repetition would give me what honesty would not. Still, in the quieter moments, when I could sit with the frustration without chasing it, I began to notice the pattern: My vagueness created vagueness. My scattered mind produced scattered pages. When I slowed down and gave shape to what I was really asking, the reflections were sharper.

That lesson bled into other parts of my life. I started listening to the way I asked questions in meetings, with family, and even in my journals. I noticed when I was rushing, when I was defensive, and when I was avoiding. Sometimes the words came out cleaner. Other times, they betrayed the same old evasions. Either way, I could see myself more clearly.

A WORD OF CAUTION

Early in my journey, I often lost track of time—working deep into the night, chasing the perfect formulation. I've described those nights honestly in this book, but I need to say plainly: They weren't healthy, and they weren't necessary.

AI can feel immersive, almost addictive. For me, it became a way to avoid stopping, to convince myself that one more prompt might unlock the clarity I craved. What I called discipline was often compulsion.

It took me a long time to change that pattern. Now I set boundaries—sessions with clear start and stop points, breaks I actually honor, and nights when I close the notebook instead of pushing through fog. The real lesson was simple but hard to accept: Reflection requires rest as much as effort.

The Intelligence Quadrant was never about magic, and it was never about the machine changing who I was. It was about training myself to face my own questions more honestly. Each iteration became a mirror—not of the AI, but of my intent clarified. That, in the end, is what "I am the I in AI" meant for me: not that the machine was alive, but that my authorship mattered.

CLOSING BRIDGE FOR CHAPTER 4

The quadrants gave me language for what had once been confusion. Business taught me the cost of illusion, family revealed the need for presence, growth showed me the grind of becoming, and intelligence reminded me to stay aligned and safe while doing it all. Together, they formed not four separate rooms, but a framework for living—a way of matching the architecture of my questions to the realities of my life.

But recognition alone wasn't enough. If I wanted the mirror to keep reflecting truth, I needed to practice. To test the framework, not as theory but as craft. And that meant putting these quadrants to work—asking better, catching drift, and building questions strong enough to hold the weight of real life.

That is where we turn next: from discovery to discipline, from recognition to practice.

PART II
METHOD

CHAPTER 5

FROM PATTERN TO PRACTICE

One night, I pushed aside the stacks of reports I had been collecting and opened my old notebooks instead. They were filled with the questions I had scribbled during months of late-night experiments. As I read through them, a strange recognition formed. The ones that had actually worked—the prompts that brought clarity instead of confusion—all seemed to share the same architecture.

At first, it felt like coincidence. But page after page confirmed it wasn't luck. I had been following a pattern without knowing it. Each time I found clarity, I had unconsciously built the question the same way.

I sat at the kitchen table with my notebooks spread wide, drawing lines between margins, circling key phrases, and sketching crude diagrams. What I saw was not just survival. It was structure. It was a framework hiding in plain sight.

That realization stopped me cold. For months, I thought I was stumbling in the dark, grateful for the rare flashes of light. But I wasn't stumbling—I was building. The pattern was repeatable. The framework could be taught.

What I discovered in those notebooks wasn't separate from the quadrants I had identified—it was the foundation beneath them. Whether I was asking business, family, growth, or intelligence questions, the same three-part structure applied.

This was the hinge. My story as a discoverer ended here. From this point forward, the focus shifts from my late nights of trial and error to a clear framework you can use for yourself.

BUILDING A PROMPT THAT WORKS

The quadrants showed me *where* questions live—business, family, growth, and intelligence. But they didn't show me *how* to build them. That's what the three-part structure reveals.

Every effective prompt, regardless of which quadrant it serves, has three essential parts: **intent, context, and form.**

- **Intent** is why you are asking.
- **Context** is the information that matters—who you are, what's at stake, and what limits apply.
- **Form** is the shape of the answer you want—a list, a plan, a table, a summary.

When these three elements are present, your prompts produce clarity instead of noise. When even one is missing, you risk vague, generic, or misleading answers.

STEP 1: INTENT

Intent is the engine of every good question. Without it, AI has no direction. With it, you give the machine a compass.

The simplest way to surface intent is to begin with **"I want…"** That phrase forces clarity.

Examples Across Quadrants

- **Business:** "I want to design a ninety-day plan to attract new real estate clients." Clear intent tells AI you're not asking for general marketing tips—you want a time-bound plan.
- **Family:** "I want to decide whether my son should attend a local college or go out of state." Stating intent prevents the answer from wandering into generic advice about higher education.
- **Growth:** "I want to learn basic Spanish before a trip in three months." Intent here sets the time frame and purpose, keeping the plan focused on travel-useful language.
- **Intelligence:** "I want to understand the risks of using AI in my small business." The "I want" signals that the answer should frame risks in a way a business owner can act on, not a researcher's technical report.

Common Failure Pattern (Missing Intent)

- Weak: "Plan a vacation."

- Better: "I want to plan a five-day relaxation vacation for two adults in Florida under $2,000."

STEP 2: CONTEXT

Context is what makes a prompt specific to *you*. It's the details AI needs to tailor the answer: who, what, where, and under what constraints.

Examples Across Quadrants

- **Business:** "My brokerage has five agents and a $5,000 monthly marketing budget." That single detail changes the scale of any suggested strategy.
- **Family:** "We are a family of four with two teenagers, traveling in July." Context prevents AI from suggesting toddler-friendly activities or winter travel destinations.
- **Growth:** "I can study thirty minutes per day, starting from zero, before I travel." Without this, the AI might assume you have hours a day or prior language knowledge.
- **Intelligence:** "I'm a small business owner with no technical background." Context ensures the AI avoids jargon and delivers practical explanations.

Common Failure Pattern (Vague Context)

- Weak: "Write me a workout plan."

- Better: "Write a four-week beginner workout plan for a forty-five-year-old with no equipment and twenty minutes a day."

STEP 3: FORM

Form tells AI the shape of the answer you want. Without it, you'll get rambling paragraphs. With it, you'll get something you can use right away.

Examples Across Quadrants

- **Business:** "Present the plan in a weekly calendar format." This makes it immediately actionable for scheduling.
- **Family:** "List three pros and three cons for each option in a table." Structure helps with side-by-side comparison.
- **Growth:** "Give me a twelve-week plan with weekly milestones." Forces AI to sequence the learning path rather than dumping random tips.
- **Intelligence:** "Summarize the five main risks in bullet points, two sentences each." Output becomes concise, digestible, and practical.

Common Failure Pattern (Missing Form)

- Weak: "Tell me about Shakespeare."
- Better: "Summarize Shakespeare's five most important plays in a bulleted list with one-sentence descriptions."

This three-part structure isn't just technique—it's protection. Every time you state clear intent, you claim authorship. Every time you provide specific context, you inject yourself into the process. Every time you define form, you shape AI to your needs rather than accepting what it offers. Intent/context/form is how you stay the "I" in "I in AI." The machine processes. You author.

Putting It Together

Here's a weak prompt: "Teach me Spanish."

Here's the same question built with the skeleton:

- **Intent:** I want to learn Spanish for travel.
- **Context:** I have thirty minutes per day to study, starting from zero, and I leave in three months.
- **Form:** Give me a twelve-week learning plan with weekly goals.

Final Prompt: "Create a twelve-week Spanish learning plan for a complete beginner preparing for travel in three months. I have thirty minutes per day to study. Present weekly goals in a table format."

The difference is immediate: The second prompt produces a plan you can actually follow. And the same skeleton works in any quadrant—for business decisions, family conversations, personal growth, or intelligence questions.

How We Actually Built Prompts

Before you practice on hypothetical scenarios, let me show you how Rebecca and I actually applied intent/context/

form in our real work. And I'll show you one of my early failures—a prompt that wasted time because I hadn't learned this structure yet.

Juan's Real Prompt (Real Estate Analysis)

Early in my PfR practice, I needed to analyze a property for a skeptical client. Before learning the structure, I would have asked "What do you think of this condo?"

After Learning Intext/Context/Form, I Built:

Intent: I want to identify the three biggest buyer hesitation points for this property.

Context: 2015 condo in Naples, FL. HOA has active litigation. Insurance premiums rose 40% last year. Target buyers are cautious locals who've been burned before. Budget-conscious, need transparency.

Form: List three hesitation points in a table: Problem / Why It Matters / How to Address It.

Final Prompt: "I want to identify the three biggest buyer hesitation points for a 2015 condo in Naples, Florida. The HOA has active litigation, insurance premiums rose 40% last year, and my target buyers are cautious locals who've been burned before. List three hesitation points in a table with columns: Problem / Why It Matters / How to Address It."

What Happened: The AI returned specific, actionable analysis I could bring directly to the client meeting. Instead of generic "condos are risky" advice, I got:

1. HOA litigation risk → buyers fear special assessments → show reserve fund health
2. Insurance volatility → monthly costs unpredictable → get 3-year rate lock quotes
3. Resale challenges → harder to sell later → price 10% below comparable non-litigation buildings

The client trusted the analysis because it matched their specific fears, not generic concerns.

REBECCA'S CREDIT CHALLENGE CLIENT

The Situation: Rebecca had a young client—call him Marcus—who wanted to buy a home for his growing family and his widowed mother. His aspiration was clear: a place big enough for everyone, a yard for his kids, and stability for his mom. But his credit history told a different story—late payments, high utilization, and collections from a business that failed. Every time he looked at his credit report, he felt defeated.

Before PfR: Rebecca asked AI: "How do I help a first-time buyer with bad credit buy a house?"

The Response: Generic advice—improve credit score, pay down debt, wait twelve to twenty-four months, consider FHA loans. True, but crushing. Marcus didn't need a checklist that reinforced why he couldn't buy yet. He needed a roadmap that showed him he could.

After Learning Intent/Context/Form:

Intent: I want to help my client buy a home for his family and widowed mother despite current credit challenges.

Context: Young father, high aspirations, challenging credit (late payments, collections), limited savings. Feels defeated when he looks at traditional timelines. Needs a motivating plan that activates his desire to achieve, not a discouraging wait-and-see approach.

Form: Create a six-month action plan broken into monthly milestones. For each month, include one credit action, one savings goal, and one family preparation step. Present as a visual roadmap showing progress toward home readiness.

Final Prompt: "I want to help my first-time homebuyer client achieve his goal of buying a home for his young family and widowed mother despite challenging credit. He has late payments, collections, and limited savings but high motivation. Create a six-month action plan with monthly milestones—each month should include one credit improvement action, one savings goal, and one family preparation step. Present as a motivating roadmap that shows measurable progress toward home readiness, not just 'wait and fix your credit.'"

What Happened:

Instead of a discouraging timeline, Rebecca got a structured plan.

Month 1–2: Foundation

- Credit action: Dispute inaccurate collection, set up autopay for current accounts.
- Savings goal: Save $200/month (start emergency fund).
- Family prep: Research neighborhoods, create family housing wishlist.

Month 3–4: Building Momentum

- Credit action: Pay down highest-utilization card, request credit limit increase on good account.
- Savings goal: Increase to $300/month, open dedicated home fund.
- Family prep: Visit model homes with family, calculate realistic monthly payment.

Month 5–6: Pre-Qualification Ready

- Credit action: Final dispute resolutions, ensure zero new inquiries.
- Savings goal: Hit $2,000 saved milestone.
- Family prep: Get prequalified, start serious house hunting.

Each milestone was achievable. Each month showed visible progress. Marcus could see himself moving toward the goal, not just being told to wait.

Rebecca's Insight:

"The form—breaking it into monthly milestones with three types of actions—was what made it work. Before, I'd tell clients 'fix your credit first,' and they'd feel hopeless. This way, Marcus could see: 'In six months, I'll be ready.' He wasn't waiting. He was building."

What changed: Marcus started working the plan immediately. By month three, his credit score had jumped forty points. By month six, he was prequalified. The plan didn't only improve his credit—it activated his belief that homeownership was possible.

WHAT *NOT* TO DO: MY EARLY PIÑATA PROMPT

Before I learned intent/context/form, I tried this:

Bad Prompt: "Give me ideas for selling condos in Florida."

What I Got: A flood of generic suggestions:

- Use social media.
- Stage the property well.
- Highlight amenities.
- Target retirees.
- Emphasize beach lifestyle.
- Consider virtual tours.
- Partner with local businesses.

The Problem: Everything and nothing. I'd sift through it, grab random pieces, and try to assemble something useful. Then I'd ask again with slight changes: "What about marketing condos?" More hits, more scattered candy.

Why It Failed:

- No intent: Was I trying to attract buyers? Write listing copy? Train agents? Plan a campaign?
- No context: Which condos? What market? What challenges? What timeline?
- No form: Did I want a list? A strategy? A script? A calendar?

The piñata method gave me activity, not progress. I was busy, but not effective.

After Learning the Structure

Intent: I want to create a sixty-day marketing campaign to sell 2015 condos with HOA challenges.

Context: Naples, Florida, market. Target buyers are cautious locals. Budget is $3,000. Need to overcome litigation fears while staying honest.

Form: Weekly action plan in table format: Week / Activity / Budget / Expected Outcome.

Result: Actionable plan I could execute Monday morning, not scattered ideas I had to sort through.

THE PATTERN YOU'LL NOTICE:

- **Juan's prompt:** Specific property, specific buyers, specific output shape → Useful analysis
- **Rebecca's prompt:** Real client, real complexity, phased structure → Clear guidance
- **Piñata prompt:** Vague everything → Scattered noise

That's the difference intent/context/form makes in real work.

WORKED EXAMPLES:

Business Quadrant

Imagine you're a real estate broker who wants to attract more clients. You know AI could help you design a plan, but you're not sure how to ask the right way.

Weak Prompt: "Help me get more clients."

The problem here is clear:

- No **intent**—What kind of help? Strategy, copywriting, social media, referrals?
- No **context**—What type of business, what market, what resources?
- No **form**—What shape should the answer take? A plan? A list? A script?

AI will return something vague like "Use social media, network, and provide good service." True, but useless.

Strong Prompt (Built Step-By-Step):

- **Intent:** "I want to design a ninety-day plan to attract new real estate clients."
- **Context:** "I am a broker in Naples, Florida, with five agents on my team and a $5,000 monthly marketing budget."
- **Form:** "Present the plan in a weekly calendar format with clear milestones."

Final Strong Prompt: "I want to design a ninety-day plan to attract new real estate clients. I am a broker in Naples, Florida, with five agents on my team and a $5,000 monthly marketing budget. Present the plan in a weekly calendar format with clear milestones."

WHY IT WORKS:

- **Intent** sets direction; it's about a plan, not random tips.
- **Context** personalizes the strategy with specific location, resources, and team size.
- **Form** ensures the answer is structured and usable right away.

What you'll receive is not generic advice, but a tailored, actionable plan you can test tomorrow.

FAMILY QUADRANT

Family decisions are often emotionally loaded, but when brought to AI, they're usually under-specified. Consider the common challenge of deciding where a teenager should attend college.

Weak Prompt: "Should my son go to a local college or out of state?"

This seems clear, but it fails structurally.

- **Intent** is fuzzy: Is the goal to compare costs, independence, or academic quality?
- **Context** is almost absent: No details about the son, the family's budget, or values.
- **Form** is missing: No instruction on how the answer should be presented for decision-making.

AI will likely give a shallow response like "Local colleges save money; out-of-state offers more independence." Technically correct, but practically useless.

Strong Prompt (Built Step-By-Step):

- **Intent:** "I want to help my son decide between attending a local college and going out of state."
- **Context:** "He is interested in medicine, we live in Florida, and our family can budget about $15,000 per year. We value both affordability and his personal growth."
- **Form:** "List the top three pros and cons of each option in a comparison table."

Final Strong Prompt: "I want to help my son decide between attending a local college and going out of state. He is interested in medicine, we live in Florida, and our family can budget about $15,000 per year. We value both affordability and his personal growth. List the top three pros and cons of each option in a comparison table."

Why It Works: This prompt frames the decision around what matters most to the family. It turns a vague either/or question into structured input that yields a side-by-side comparison, something they can bring to the dinner table and discuss together.

GROWTH QUADRANT

Growth questions often start with ambition but collapse into vagueness when asked of AI. Take the classic case of learning a new language.

Weak Prompt: "Teach me Spanish."

This is too broad.

- **Intent** isn't specified—do you want conversation skills, travel basics, or academic fluency?
- **Context** is missing—what's your starting level, how much time do you have, and why are you learning?
- **Form** is absent—what structure should the instruction take?

AI will reply with scattered vocabulary lists or grammar explanations. Without guidance, the result is overwhelming and hard to follow.

Strong Prompt (Built Step-By-Step):

- **Intent:** "I want to learn Spanish for travel."
- **Context:** "I'm a complete beginner, I leave in three months, and I can study thirty minutes per day."
- **Form:** "Create a twelve-week plan with weekly goals in table format."

Final Strong Prompt: "I want to learn Spanish for travel. I'm a complete beginner, I leave in three months, and I can study thirty minutes per day. Create a twelve-week plan with weekly goals in table format."

Why It Works: This transforms a vague request into a time-bound study plan, matched to both purpose (travel) and constraint (time available). The table format turns it into a schedule a learner can actually follow. Instead of loose tips, the reader gets a roadmap with milestones.

INTELLIGENCE QUADRANT

When exploring intelligence or technology questions, people often fall into the trap of asking in abstract terms. For example, a small business owner may want to understand the risks of AI but pose the question too generally.

Weak Prompt: "What are the risks of AI?"

This fails because:

- **Intent** is absent—does the person want ethical risks, business risks, or technical risks?

- **Context** is missing—what kind of business, what level of expertise?
- **Form** is undefined—should the risks be listed, explained in detail, or compared?

AI will likely produce a generic essay about privacy, bias, and job loss. Interesting, but not directly useful.

Strong Prompt (Built Step-By-Step):

- **Intent:** "I want to understand the risks of using AI in my small business."
- **Context:** "I run a local retail shop with ten employees. I have no technical background, but I'm considering using AI for marketing and customer service."
- **Form:** "Summarize the five most important risks in bullet points, with each explained in two sentences."

Final Strong Prompt: "I want to understand the risks of using AI in my small business. I run a local retail shop with ten employees. I have no technical background, but I'm considering using AI for marketing and customer service. Summarize the five most important risks in bullet points, with each explained in two sentences."

Why It Works: This prompt ensures the AI's response will be practical, accessible, and tailored to a specific business context. Instead of abstract risks, the owner will get a concise list directly tied to their situation, written in plain language they can act on.

TROUBLESHOOTING: COMMON MISTAKES WHEN BUILDING PROMPTS

Even with a clear framework, beginners often stumble in predictable ways. Below are six common mistakes and how to fix them.

Mistake #1: Missing Intent

- Weak Prompt: "Plan a vacation."
- Problem: AI has no idea what kind of vacation you want—relaxation, adventure, family, or luxury.
- Fix: Add "I want…" to surface purpose.
- Better Prompt: "I want to plan a five-day family vacation focused on relaxation in Florida under $2,000."

Mistake #2: Vague Context

- Weak Prompt: "Write a workout plan."
- Problem: Without age, fitness level, or time available, AI guesses—and usually misses.
- Fix: Provide relevant details that shape the plan.
- Better Prompt: "Write a four-week beginner workout plan for a forty-five-year-old with twenty minutes a day and no equipment."

Mistake #3: Irrelevant Detail

- Weak Prompt: "Write a speech for my company's tenth anniversary. We'll serve chicken parmesan at dinner, and the venue has blue curtains."
- Problem: Extra details (menu, curtain color) don't affect the output but distract the AI.
- Fix: Strip away noise; keep only context that changes the answer.
- Better Prompt: "Write a five-minute speech for my company's tenth anniversary, focusing on customer gratitude and team milestones."

Mistake #4: Missing Form

- Weak Prompt: "Tell me about Shakespeare."
- Problem: The AI may ramble in long paragraphs.
- Fix: Specify the desired output shape.
- Better Prompt: "Summarize Shakespeare's five most important plays in a bulleted list with one-sentence descriptions."

Mistake #5: Stacking Multiple Intents

- Weak Prompt: "Write me a business plan, marketing strategy, and website copy for my new bakery."
- Problem: Three different jobs, one overloaded prompt. AI will produce shallow results.
- Fix: Break the request into separate prompts, each with one clear intent.

- Better Prompt: "I want a ninety-day marketing plan to attract local customers for my new bakery."

Mistake #6: Forgetting Audience Alignment

- Weak Prompt: "Explain blockchain."
- Problem: AI may deliver a technical essay when you need a simple analogy.
- Fix: Specify audience in context.
- Better Prompt: "Explain blockchain to a group of high school students using a simple analogy."

TAKEAWAY

Most prompt failures aren't because AI is "broken." They happen when Intent, Context, or Form is unclear, missing, or misapplied. Strip out irrelevant noise, focus on one intent at a time, and always shape the answer to your audience.

NOW YOUR TURN

You've seen how we actually used this in real estate. Now practice on the scenarios below, knowing that this structure works in real life, not only in theory.

Practice: Build Your Own Prompts

It's one thing to read examples—it's another to try it yourself. Use these practice scenarios to apply the intent/context/form structure. After you write your version, compare it to the sample solution. Don't worry if your answer isn't identical; what matters is whether all three parts are present and clear.

Scenario 1: Business

You're launching a new bakery and want to design a first-month marketing plan.

- **Your Turn:** Write a prompt using intent, context, and form.
- **Sample Solution:**
    - **Intent:** "I want to design a marketing plan for the first thirty days of my bakery."
    - **Context:** "The bakery is in a small town, I have a $2,000 budget, and I want to focus on local customers."
    - **Form:** "Present the plan in a four-week calendar format."
    - **Final Prompt:** "I want to design a marketing plan for the first thirty days of my bakery. The bakery is in a small town, I have a $2,000 budget, and I want to focus on local customers. Present the plan in a four-week calendar format."

Scenario 2: Family

You're planning a family reunion for twenty people over a weekend.

- **Your Turn:** Write a prompt using intent, context, and form.

- **Sample Solution:**
  - **Intent:** "I want to plan a weekend schedule for a family reunion."
  - **Context:** "We'll have twenty relatives, ages five to seventy, and the event is in Orlando."
  - **Form:** "Create a two-day schedule in table format with meals, activities, and free time."
  - **Final Prompt:** "I want to plan a weekend schedule for a family reunion. We'll have twenty relatives, ages five to seventy, and the event is in Orlando. Create a two-day schedule in table format with meals, activities, and free time."

Scenario 3: Growth

You want to build confidence in public speaking over the next month.

- **Your Turn:** Write a prompt using Intent, Context, and Form.
- **Sample Solution:**
  - **Intent:** "I want to build confidence in public speaking."
  - **Context:** "I have one month before a presentation, I'm a beginner, and I can practice fifteen minutes daily."
  - **Form:** "Design a four-week practice plan with daily exercises listed in a table."

- **Final Prompt:** "I want to build confidence in public speaking. I have one month before a presentation, I'm a beginner, and I can practice fifteen minutes daily. Design a four-week practice plan with daily exercises listed in a table."

Reflection (Continued): Compare your prompts with these examples. Did you clearly state **intent**, provide specific **context**, and define a usable **form**? If so, you've built strong prompts ready to test in real life. If not, revisit your wording. Small adjustments—clarifying purpose, adding relevant detail, shaping the output—can make the difference between a vague response and a clear, actionable answer.

PROGRESSION: FROM FRAMEWORK TO VOICE

At first, you'll lean on the skeleton—intent, context, and form—like training wheels. That's expected. But strong prompting isn't about memorizing my examples. It's about building a way of asking that reflects *you*.
Think of it in stages:

Stage 1: Structured Basics

You follow the framework exactly: "I want.../Here's my situation/Give it to me in this shape." It feels mechanical, but it works.

Stage 2: Personal Refinement

You begin adding your own voice: words you'd actually use with a colleague, values that matter to you, priorities that make the answer yours. The structure fades into the background as your identity comes forward.

Stage 3: Adaptive Identity
Your prompts now reflect perspective, not only structure. A parent frames questions around family growth. A business owner highlights customer trust. A student builds curiosity into their phrasing. AI doesn't just process words—it mirrors your identity in the response.

Stage 4: Mastery

You no longer think about intent, context, and form as separate steps. You craft questions naturally, blending clarity with your personal style. The framework lives inside your way of asking, like grammar in a fluent conversation.

EXAMPLE OF PROGRESSION:

- **Stage 1 (basic):** "I want a ninety-day marketing plan. My bakery is in a small town with a $2,000 budget. Present the plan in a weekly calendar."
- **Stage 2 (refined):** "I'm opening a bakery in a small town, and my budget is only $2,000. Help me build a ninety-day plan that emphasizes word-of-mouth and community loyalty, laid out week by week."
- **Stage 3 (identity-driven):** "This bakery is my way of honoring my grandmother's recipes. With a $2,000 budget and a ninety-day runway, show me how to build a loyal local following through

community-driven marketing. Put it in a calendar I can follow."

Takeaway

The skeleton gives you stability, but your identity gives it power. The real goal isn't to build better prompts—it's to build prompts that sound like you. Once your way of asking reflects your way of being, AI becomes more than a tool. It becomes a mirror of your intent and a partner in your growth.

WHAT COMES NEXT

Once you've built your prompt using **intent, context, and form**, you have a foundation that works. But foundation alone isn't enough. The next step is learning how to evaluate what comes back—how to recognize when an answer is useful versus when it's vague, generic, or misleading. That's where calibration begins, and that's what we'll explore in the next chapter.

CHAPTER 6

CALIBRATION—EVALUATING WHAT COMES BACK

6A: OPENING: WHEN GOOD PROMPTS AREN'T ENOUGH

I thought I had mastered the game. After months of trial and error, I had learned to build prompts that worked—clear intent, relevant context, and defined form. My questions felt sharp, my directions precise. Yet one client meeting reminded me how fragile that confidence was. I had prepared for weeks to deliver a presentation to a large non-profit organization. After preparing using my AI prompting tactics, I was ready.

But during the client meeting, my confidence unraveled. One board member, after the presentation, said, "Frankly, we could generate something like this ourselves." That stung hard; my presentation failed to deliver any real insight or added value. Instead of influencing decisions or moving strategy forward, my work simply mirrored what was already possible for them. The lesson was clear: Relevance and impact matter far more than a slick presentation.

Worse, it quickly became clear that my analysis offered no real advantage over what the team already knew or could do themselves. Instead of clarifying strategy or bringing fresh insight, it felt like I had simply repackaged public information. At that moment, my expertise—and the AI's output—seemed less relevant, and my contribution fell flat.

The problem wasn't the prompt. The problem was me. I had treated the first fluent answer as the absolute truth, assuming clarity on the front end guaranteed quality on the back end. It didn't. I hadn't calibrated.

That day, I realized a painful lesson: **Asking well is only half the work. The other half is learning to judge what comes back.** AI can sound confident while being vague. It can structure information cleanly while drifting from your actual question. It can produce eloquence without evidence. And if you don't have a way to evaluate the response, you risk carrying illusion into decisions that matter.

I encountered a similar issue preparing content for a legal research presentation. I asked an AI tool to summarize regulations relevant to condominium compliance policy. The output was impressive at first glance—thorough explanations, neatly organized statutes, and citations that looked authoritative.

However, when I cross-checked the information, I realized some statutory references were outdated and a few interpretations didn't align with the current law. The AI had composed a presentation that appeared comprehensive, but several key points failed the accuracy test. If I had relied on it without careful validation, I could have presented misleading or even incorrect legal references.

That experience underscored a vital lesson: While AI can generate structured content rapidly, it's up to us to verify every detail—especially when accuracy means referring directly to the statute itself. The answer may look convincing, but its trustworthiness must be earned through diligent validation. Here's an example using your legal research scenario:

I ran into the same challenge while preparing a presentation for a legal research project. I relied on an AI tool to outline a new regulatory framework, complete with language from relevant statutes and summaries of recent case law. The slides came out neat and comprehensive, as if ready for a courtroom.

But before presenting, I double-checked the citations and statutory references. Several turned out to be outdated, and one summary misstated the actual legal requirements. The AI-generated material felt complete, yet without validation against the actual statute, it was misleading.

That experience reinforced an important truth: AI will always provide a result, but accuracy—especially in law—demands careful human review and corroboration with the real statute. It's not enough for the answer to look right; it must be proven right.

These moments taught me something crucial: **AI will always give you an answer. But whether that answer deserves your trust—that's your job.**

I began thinking of it like a job interview. A résumé may look polished, but the interview reveals what really matters.

Does this person actually know what they claim? Can they apply their skills to real situations? Do they align with your team's values? A prompt is the résumé. Calibration is the interview. You wouldn't hire based only on the résumé. Why would you trust an AI response without testing it?

From that point forward, I built a second layer into my process—not only construction but evaluation. I needed a way to hold up the output like a mirror and ask:

- Does this reflect my real intent?
- Does it carry my voice, or did I hand authorship to the machine?
- Does it have substance, or just the illusion of clarity?
- Does it align with my values and the identity I'm trying to build?

Those four questions became the quality checks that changed everything for me. They caught drift before it misled me, restored my voice where it had slipped away, exposed empty answers that looked good on the surface, and reminded me that even useful output wasn't worth much if it contradicted who I wanted to be.

Calibration isn't about nitpicking or chasing perfection. It's about confidence—the confidence to act knowing you've tested what's in front of you. Without it, you risk mistaking eloquence for truth. With it, you can trust both your process and your decisions.

That was the moment I realized I needed to calibrate—not simply to ask well, but to judge what came back. The next sections break down the four quality checks that make calibration possible.

6B: THE FOUR QUALITY CHECKS

Building good prompts is only half the craft. The other half is learning to judge the answers. Calibration means applying four quality checks that filter noise, protect your voice, ground results in truth, and ensure alignment with your deeper values.

MIRROR & SIGNAL CHECK

Definition

The first test asks: Does this answer reflect my actual intent, or has it drifted into noise?

AI is prone to filling gaps with generic patterns. Even if you built a clear prompt, the output can veer toward what's common rather than what you specifically asked. Mirror & Signal means holding the response up like a mirror. Does it reflect the signal of your request, or is it echoing background static?

Cross-Quadrant Examples

- **Business:** You say "Design a ninety-day plan for attracting new clients with a $5,000 monthly marketing budget." AI replies with "Use social media, provide excellent service, and consider networking events." True statements, but they ignore the budget and time frame. That's drift.

Fix: Reassert your intent. "Focus only on tactics that can be executed within a $5,000 monthly budget, broken down by week."

- **Family:** You say "List pros and cons of my son attending college in-state versus out-of-state." AI responds with a broad essay on the benefits of higher education. The intent—comparison of two options—is missing.

  Fix: Remind the system: "Provide a side-by-side table, not a general essay."

- **Growth:** You say "Create a twelve-week Spanish study plan for a beginner with thirty minutes a day." AI replies with random vocabulary lists and grammar rules, but no weekly sequence. The signal (structured plan) has been lost.

  Fix: Specify: "Organize by week, with cumulative milestones."

- **Intelligence:** You say "Summarize risks of using AI in my small business in plain language." AI generates a dense report full of jargon and regulatory citations. The signal (plain language) is missing.

  Fix: Clarify: "Explain as if to a nontechnical business owner."

SELF-CHECK QUESTIONS

1. Does this answer address my *specific* request, or is it drifting into what's most common?

2. Am I seeing my intent clearly mirrored back, or just vague platitudes?
3. If drift is happening, which part of my intent was ignored?

Fix: Reassert intent directly in the next prompt. Calibration often means repeating yourself with sharper focus.

AUTHORSHIP CHECK

Definition

The second test asks: Am I letting AI generate ideas that should come from me?

AI is a processor, not a replacement for your imagination or lived experience. If you hand over authorship, you risk polished text that lacks your voice and credibility. The Authorship Check keeps you—not the machine—at the creative center.

Cross-Quadrant Examples

- **Business:** You say "Write a client outreach email." AI produces a slick but generic message: "We value your business and look forward to working with you." It could be from any company.

  Fix: Inject your authentic phrasing: "As a Naples broker who grew up here, I want to help you find not just a house but a place that feels like home."
- **Family:** You say "Draft a message to my son about choosing a college." AI gives you: "Dear student,

choosing a college is an important decision for your future." That's sterile.

Fix: Add personal authorship: "Your mother and I remember how we felt leaving home at eighteen—excited and scared. We'll support you either way."

- **Growth:** You say "Write a personal reflection on learning Spanish." AI gives you clichés about "expanding horizons."

  Fix: Inject your story: "When I first tried to order dinner in Madrid and stumbled over the menu, I laughed so hard the waiter joined in. That moment taught me learning can be fun, not just serious."

- **Intelligence:** You say "Summarize ethical risks of AI." AI provides polished corporate-speak.

  Fix: Inject your stake: "As a small business owner, my concern isn't theoretical bias—it's whether an AI tool might mishandle my clients' personal data."

SELF-CHECK

- Does this sound like *me*, or like a brochure?
- Are the key examples drawn from my life or generic filler?
- Would my client, family, or colleague recognize my voice in this?

Fix: Add one authentic detail or phrase that only you could provide. Let AI structure around it, but don't give away authorship.

TRUTH VERSUS ILLUSION CHECK

Definition

The third test asks: Does this answer contain verifiable substance, or just eloquent illusion?

AI often generates responses that sound fluent but lack grounding. This is "hallucination" in technical terms. Truth versus Illusion is about demanding evidence, numbers, or anchors that tether the answer to reality.

Cross-Quadrant Examples

- **Business:** You ask "What's the ROI of direct mail in real estate?"
- **AI answer:** "Direct mail is highly effective at reaching potential buyers." Sounds good, but no numbers.

  Fix: Demand: "Cite industry benchmarks with specific percentages from credible sources."
- **Family:** You ask "What are the long-term effects of out-of-state college?"
- **AI response:** "Students who attend out of state often broaden their horizons." That's vague

Fix: Say "Provide data on graduation rates and average student debt for in-state versus out-of-state."

- **Growth:** You say "Best methods for learning Spanish quickly."

  AI reply: "Practice consistently, immerse yourself, and use apps." True but empty.

  Fix: Require: "List three peer-reviewed studies or statistics on language acquisition speed."

- **Intelligence:** You ask "What are the risks of AI adoption in small businesses?"
- **AI response:** "There are ethical and operational risks." Meaningless without examples.

  Fix: Say "List five risks with real-world case studies from small businesses."

SELF-CHECK

- Are claims supported by data or case examples?
- Could I verify this answer independently?
- Does the response avoid specifics where they matter most?

Fix: Demand specificity—numbers, sources, or examples.

CONSISTENCY CHECK

Definition

The final test asks: Is this output aligned with my values and long-term goals?

Sometimes AI gives answers that are factually correct and well-structured but inconsistent with your identity. Calibration means ensuring consistency between the immediate output and your larger principles.

Cross-Quadrant Examples

- **Business:** You ask "How can I scale my brokerage?"
- AI suggests cutting staff and outsourcing. Technically viable, but inconsistent with your value of building a loyal team.

  Fix: Add: "Propose strategies that preserve and grow staff opportunities."
- **Family:** You ask "What's the best way to balance work and parenting?"
- AI suggests outsourcing childcare entirely. That might optimize efficiency but clash with your desire to be present as a parent.

  Fix: Add: "Include options that maximize my direct time with my kids."
- **Growth:** You ask "How do I accelerate Spanish learning?"
- AI recommends eight hours a day of immersion. Effective, but impossible given your schedule and health.

  Fix: Add: "Constrain to thirty minutes per day, sustainable pace."
- **Intelligence:** You ask "How do I adopt AI in my business?"

- AI suggests aggressive data collection. That may work, but it violates your privacy standards.

  Fix: Add: "Ensure recommendations respect client confidentiality."

SELF-CHECK

- Does this advice serve my long-term identity, not just short-term goals?
- Would following this make me proud of the outcome?
- Does this align with how I want to be seen by clients, family, or myself?

Fix: Include explicit value statements in your prompts so outputs don't just solve problems, but solve them *your way*.

SUMMARY OF 6B

These four checks—Mirror & Signal, Authorship, Truth versus Illusion, and Consistency—form the calibration toolkit. Together, they prevent drift, keep your voice central, demand substance, and align results with who you are. Even the best-constructed prompt needs this second layer of judgment. Without it, you risk mistaking fluent noise for useful truth.

6B-2: HOW WE ACTUALLY CALIBRATED

These aren't theoretical examples. They're the moments when calibration saved me from embarrassment, helped Rebecca connect with a struggling client, and taught me that "looks good" is never good enough.

JUAN'S MARKET ANALYSIS: WHEN I TRUSTED WITHOUT CHECKING

I thought I had it figured out. After months of practice, I could build strong prompts. Intent, context, form—I knew the drill. So when I asked AI for a market analysis on a Naples condo, I trusted the output. It came back polished: comp properties, price trends, graphs, bullet points. Professional. Ready to present.

I printed it. Brought it to the client meeting. Set it on the table with confidence.

Then my colleague glanced at the numbers and frowned. "These comps aren't even in the same school district," she said. Another person pointed out that one of the price trends contradicted county records. My face burned. I had carried noise into a professional room.

What I Did Wrong: The prompt was strong. The output looked good. But I never ran the checks.

Mirror & Signal: I asked for "comparable sales" but didn't specify what made properties truly comparable—same school district, same HOA structure, similar age.

Authorship: The language was generic broker-speak. Could've been anyone, anywhere.

Truth versus Illusion: This was the killer. No sources. No verification. I assumed "AI said it" meant "it's true." Wrong.

Consistency: I preach "credibility over speed" but rushed this analysis because it looked professional.

What I Learned: After that meeting, I built one simple habit: Before I present any analysis, I verify one key claim. Just one.

In this case, I now check "Are these comps actually in the same school district?" If I can't verify it in sixty seconds on the county website, it doesn't go in the presentation.

That's it. Not a ten-step protocol. Just verify the claim that would embarrass me most if it's wrong.

The Fix: My new prompt includes one line: "List the school district for each comp. I'll verify before presenting."

That one detail changed everything. Now, when I present, I know the foundation is solid.

REBECCA'S EMAIL: WHEN THE WORDS WERE RIGHT BUT THE VOICE WAS WRONG

Rebecca had a client who was drowning. He was a first-time waterfront buyer trying to figure out zoning for a fishing business and short-term rentals. He had insurance questions and faced financing confusion. He was overwhelmed.

She asked AI to draft an email explaining the three phases he needed to tackle. The output came back fast: "Thank you for your interest in waterfront property acquisition. Please find below the structured process for your consideration: Phase 1: Zoning Verification—Confirm municipal compliance..."

Rebecca almost hit send. Then she stopped. "This doesn't sound like me at all."

WHAT SHE CAUGHT:

Mirror & Signal: → The three phases were there.

Authorship: → "Municipal compliance"? "Liability parameters"? This sounded like a bank form letter. Her brand was "I listen more than I talk. I care if you're happy." This email was cold.

Truth versus Illusion: → The phases were accurate.

Consistency: → Her whole identity is patience. This email felt rushed and corporate.

Her Fix: She rewrote it in ten minutes, using her actual voice.

> "Hi [Client],
>
> I know looking at waterfront properties feels overwhelming right now—there's a lot to figure out. Let's take this one step at a time.
>
> First: We'll check if the zoning allows both your fishing business and short-term rentals. Once that's clear, we'll tackle insurance. Then financing.
>
> You don't have to understand everything at once. That's what I'm here for.
>
> Want to talk about zoning this week?
>
> Rebecca"

What Happened: Her client responded within an hour: "This is exactly what I needed to hear. Let's talk Thursday."

The Lesson: Rebecca's takeaway was simple: "The AI version was correct. But my version was me. Calibration taught me that accuracy isn't enough if you don't sound human."

Now, before she sends any AI-drafted message, she asks herself one question: "Would I actually say this out loud to someone sitting across from me?"

If no, she rewrites.

THE LISTING DESCRIPTION: WHEN THREE CHECKS PASSED BUT ONE FAILED

Early in my practice, I asked AI to write a listing description for a waterfront condo. The output was beautiful—poetic language, compelling narrative, professional polish:

"Waterfront luxury living with private beach access. Wake up to ocean breezes and sunset views from your expansive balcony..."

I read it. Thought, *Perfect*. Posted it to the MLS immediately.

Two days later, a client called. "Your listing says beach access. I drove by—it's two miles inland."

My stomach dropped. The condo had a water view of a canal. No beach. No ocean access. The AI had hallucinated "beach access," and I had published it as fact.

WHAT I MISSED:

Mirror & Signal: → Addressed the property.

Authorship: → Sounded professional.

Truth versus Illusion:→ "Beach access"—completely false. "Ocean breezes"—it faced a canal. "Sunset views"—the balcony faced east.

Consistency: → Aligned with my goal of attractive listings.

The Mistake: I saw three checks passing and thought that was good enough. It wasn't. One failed Truth check destroyed everything else.

What I Do Now: Before I post any listing, I verify the one claim buyers care about most. In this case: access. Does this property actually have beach access, or just a view? I check the deed. It only takes two minutes and saves credibility.

My new prompt includes: "Do not mention beach access, ocean views, or sunset views unless I provide documentation. Describe only what's verifiable: canal view, east-facing balcony."

The Lesson: "Looks good" doesn't mean "it's true." Now I assume every specific claim is wrong until I verify it myself.

THE PATTERN

Three stories, three different failures:

Story	What Failed	Result	The Fix
Market Analysis	Truth (no sources)	Professional embarrassment	Verify one key claim before presenting
Rebecca's Email	Authorship (corporate voice)	Almost sent cold message	Ask "Would I say this out loud?"
Listing	Truth (false claims)	Published misinformation	Check the claim buyers care about most

Notice the fixes aren't complicated. They're simple habits:

Verify one claim

Read it aloud

Check the thing that matters most

That's calibration. Not perfection. Just protection.

THE LAW

If any check fails, stop.

You can't compensate for missing truth with better style. You can't bypass drift with polish. All four checks matter.

When calibration catches a problem, fix it before you ship it. That's the difference between confident action and careless mistakes.

Now let's see how these four checks work on a complete example, step-by-step.

6C: WORKED EXAMPLE: APPLYING ALL FOUR CHECKS

In Chapter 5, you built a strong prompt for your bakery marketing plan.

Prompt: "I want to design a ninety-day plan to attract new clients for my bakery. The bakery is in a small town, I have a $2,000 budget, and I want to focus on local customers. Present the plan in a twelve-week calendar format with clear weekly milestones."

This had intent, context, and form. But construction alone isn't enough. Let's see how calibration works when you apply all four checks.

THE RAW AI OUTPUT

Weeks 1–4: Post on social media three times per week. Offer discounts. Print flyers for local distribution.

Weeks 5–8: Run Facebook ads, host one in-store event. Continue social media.

Weeks 9–12: Collect customer feedback, expand advertising, plan seasonal promotion.

Budget: $1,200 for ads, $500 for flyers, $300 for event.

This looks plausible—clear tasks and a budget breakdown. But it misses the mark in subtle ways. Calibration reveals the gaps.

1. Mirror & Signal Check

Does this reflect my actual intent?

You asked for a *weekly calendar with milestones*. Instead, you got three broad phases. That's drift.

Correction: Reassert intent.

"Provide a detailed twelve-week calendar with two to three specific activities per week. Include one community-facing activity per week."

The revision now breaks down into weekly goals instead of vague clusters. Calibration tightened the mirror.

2. Authorship Check

Does this preserve my voice?

The revised calendar lists "generic social media posts" and "local discount offers." These could belong to any bakery. Nothing reflects your story, your recipes, or why people should choose you.

Correction: Inject authorship.

"Incorporate my bakery's identity: emphasize my grandmother's recipes, highlight local ingredients, and use a warm, community-centered tone."

The new version suggests:

- Week 2: Launch a "grandmother's recipe spotlight" on social media.
- Week 6: Host a "story-sharing night" at the bakery.
- Week 10: Partner with the local school fundraiser.

Your voice is now present.

3. Truth versus Illusion Check

Does this contain real substance?

The plan still floats on generalities. $1,200 for ads—what does that buy? What reach can you expect? Without benchmarks, the advice is illusion, not truth.

Correction: Demand evidence.

"Provide cost-per-engagement estimates, expected impressions for $1,200 in ads, and conversion benchmarks from similar small-town bakeries."

Now the plan shows:

- $1,200 = ~15,000 impressions on Facebook, estimated $0.08 per engagement.
- Flyers: $0.25 per household, expected 3% response rate.
- Referral discount: 10% uptake average.

This gives you numbers you can test, not just ideas.

4. Consistency Check

Is this aligned with my values and goals?
The numbers are stronger, but the plan leans heavily on paid ads and discounts. That may attract traffic, but it risks diluting your identity as a trusted, community-rooted bakery.

Correction: Anchor values.

"Revise to limit flyers to five hundred, cap ads at $1,000, and ensure each week includes a relationship-building activity."

The final version shifts:

- Flyers reduced to five hundred, targeting homes within walking distance.
- Ads capped at $1,000 with precise targeting.
- Weekly community touches: recipe-sharing posts, farmers market booth, school partnerships.

Now the plan respects both your budget and your principle of building loyalty over time.

THE FINAL CALIBRATED OUTPUT

Week 1: Social post introducing bakery's origin story. $100 local ad.

Week 2: "Grandmother's recipe spotlight" campaign.

Week 3: Deliver five hundred flyers to nearby homes.

Week 4: Host "bread and story" evening.

Week 5: Launch referral program ("Bring a friend, get 10% off").

Week 6: Story-sharing night at bakery.

Week 7: Partner with local school fundraiser.

Week 8: $200 targeted ad, expected three thousand impressions.

Week 9: Seasonal promotion tied to town event.

Week 10: "Kids decorate cupcakes" workshop.

Week 11: Booth at farmers market.

Week 12: Gather feedback, share results, plan next cycle.

Budget: $1,000 for ads, $200 for flyers, $300 for events.

WHY THIS MATTERS

Notice the progression:

- **Mirror & Signal** caught drift and forced weekly detail.
- **Authorship** restored personal story.
- **Truth versus Illusion** demanded numbers and evidence.
- **Consistency** aligned the plan with long-term values.

The final plan isn't perfect—it never will be—but it's usable, specific, and true to your identity.

KEY TAKEAWAY

Construction (intent/context/form) gives you the skeleton. Calibration (four checks) strengthens it into something you can trust and act on.

These checks exist because democratized intelligence means everyone has access to AI, but access without discernment creates dependency. Mirror & Signal keeps you from drifting. Authorship keeps you from disappearing. Truth versus Illusion keeps you grounded. Consistency keeps you aligned with who you're becoming. Calibration is how you ensure AI amplifies your intelligence rather than replacing it.

6D: PRACTICE EXERCISES

Reading examples teaches principles. Applying them makes them stick. Below are two practice scenarios. Try them yourself before reading the sample analyses.

Remember: Calibration is rarely neat. Problems overlap, and different readers may choose different valid corrections. The goal isn't perfection—it's improvement that makes the answer usable.

EXERCISE 1: BUSINESS QUADRANT (STRAIGHTFORWARD)

Prompt: "I want a four-week social media calendar to promote my yoga studio. Context: $500 budget, focus on attracting young professionals. Form: weekly table with post ideas."

Raw Output: "Promote your classes online. Offer discounts for new members. Encourage people to join. Track your results."

Your Turn: Apply the four checks.

Sample Analysis:

- **Mirror & Signal:** Drift. You asked for a weekly table, got generic prose. → Correction: Demand tabular format with specific weekly tasks.
- **Authorship:** Generic language ("encourage people") doesn't sound like your studio. → Correction: Inject your voice ("invite people to destress after work with yoga flow classes").
- **Truth versus Illusion:** No substance about cost or reach. → Correction: Require expected ad spend per week and engagement estimates.
- **Consistency:** Heavy on discounts may clash with premium positioning. → Correction: Request activities that build brand trust (testimonials, workplace wellness tie-ins).

EXERCISE 2: FAMILY QUADRANT (NUANCED)

Prompt: "I want a side-by-side comparison of summer activities for my two teenagers: local science camp versus study-abroad program. Include costs, risks, and benefits."

Raw Output: "Science camps are affordable and fun. Study abroad offers independence and cultural learning. Both options have advantages."

At first glance, this seems fine—it names both options and highlights differences. But calibration reveals more.

Sample Analysis:

- **Mirror & Signal:** Drift: You asked for a side-by-side comparison with costs/risks/benefits. Instead, you got a paragraph. → Correction: Demand a table format.
- **Authorship:** Output reads like a brochure. Your family's concerns—safety, distance, staying connected—are absent. → Correction: Add "Include notes on safety and family impact, not just general benefits."
- **Truth versus Illusion:** Vague claims ("affordable," "offers independence") without numbers. → Correction: Require actual cost ranges ($1,500–$2,000 camp versus $6,000+ abroad).
- **Consistency:** Advice doesn't check against values. If your family prioritizes close bonds, study abroad may conflict. → Correction: Add constraint: "Highlight how each option affects family connection."

REFLECTION

Notice the difference between the two exercises.

- In **Exercise 1**, the flaws were obvious. The output ignored form, skipped specifics, and sounded generic. Calibration was straightforward.
- In **Exercise 2**, the output looked acceptable at first, but calibration revealed subtle problems—missing numbers, absent voice, misaligned values.

This mirrors real practice. Sometimes the issues are glaring. Other times, they're hidden in what looks polished. Calibration helps you catch both.

6E: WHEN TO ITERATE VERSUS WHEN TO STOP

One of the hidden risks of calibration is getting stuck. Once you see how much a prompt can improve through refinement, it's tempting to keep iterating endlessly—demanding sharper numbers, tighter phrasing, and more polished outputs. But calibration isn't about chasing perfection. It's about reaching a point where the answer is reliable enough to act on.

SIGNS YOU NEED ANOTHER ITERATION

- **Still vague:** The output speaks in generalities. "Use social media" instead of "Spend $200 on three Facebook ads targeting local families."
- **Misaligned:** The plan solves the wrong problem or ignores your core values. You asked for a family-friendly approach and got "outsource childcare completely."
- **Missing evidence:** Claims sound plausible but carry no data, benchmarks, or real-world examples.
- **Voice off:** The answer reads like generic filler, not in your tone or perspective.

If you see one or more of these, run another cycle. Adjust the prompt, reassert your intent, and push the system closer to what you need.

SIGNS YOU SHOULD STOP

- **Specific:** The answer gives clear steps, numbers, or structures you can test.
- **Actionable:** You know what to do next—plan a meeting, test an ad, schedule an event.
- **Aligned:** The output fits your values and long-term direction.
- **Good enough:** It may not be perfect, but it's useful right now.

When these signs appear, it's time to stop refining and start acting. Every iteration costs time. If each cycle yields only minor cosmetic improvements, you've crossed the line from calibration into perfectionism.

THE HEALTH-CONSCIOUS BOUNDARY

"Good enough for decision-making beats endless polishing." That's the rule. The point of democratized intelligence isn't to produce flawless documents—it's to help you think clearly and act confidently. AI should accelerate your momentum, not trap you in revision.

Calibration is about reliability, not perfection. It ensures you don't mistake eloquent noise for truth, but it also reminds you that progress requires moving forward. Knowing when to stop is as much a skill as knowing how to build.

6F: BRIDGE TO CHAPTER 7

You now know how to build prompts that work and calibrate the answers that come back. With intent, context, and form, you create. With the four checks, you judge. Together, these tools keep you in authorship while using AI's processing power.

The next step is recursion—applying this cycle across increasingly complex challenges. In Chapter 7, we'll see how building, calibrating, and refining in loops can deepen clarity, strengthen alignment, and help you tackle decisions that no single prompt can resolve in one pass.

CHAPTER 7

ITERATION

I used to believe intelligence meant answering quickly—the faster the decision, the stronger the leader. But as my responsibilities and projects multiplied, that belief began to erode.

7A: OPENING

It happened during a season when my business was poised for a leap. Opportunities kept coming: travel, expansion, more staff, and the promise of bigger profits. The proposals glittered with charts and confident projections, urging me to seize the next step without hesitation.

But night after night, I found myself walking through the door far later than before. My wife would be in the kitchen, finishing dinner in the quiet hum of the house. The routine—her cooking, the anticipation of a shared meal—became a gentle reminder of what anchored my life. Each evening, I'd see the warmth in the kitchen, but also realize how much more often I was missing it.

Growth, once so alluring, began to take on the shape of absence: lost time, missed moments, a house that still welcomed me but reflected my distance. "Presence, not presents," she once said. That stuck.

That was the start of my first recursive loop. The question shifted from "Should I expand?" to "Can I expand without sacrificing this?" The calculus changed with every late arrival—every dinner where I was just another guest.

I thought about it constantly, running numbers and what-ifs, but the answer kept slipping away. The tension grew stronger with every new commitment, every flight, every night spent away from what mattered most.

One evening, during a quiet conversation as she finished in the kitchen, my wife looked up and said, "You don't have to build more just to prove yourself. Consider what you're leaving behind to chase what's ahead."

Her words cut through the noise. It wasn't only about business—it was about the life we'd built together and how each decision threatened to compress the time that gave it meaning.

Now, as I take on more projects and travel expands my horizon but compresses my time, I realize true leadership isn't about quick answers but about asking which loops are worth living—and which life I might be leaving behind.

7B: WHY ITERATION MATTERS

I used to think clarity was about striking gold on the first swing. Ask a sharp question, get a sharp answer, and move on. For years, I treated both business and family decisions that way—quick, decisive, done. But I learned the hard way that most first answers don't carry enough weight to last.

The machine made this visible. Type a vague prompt—*Tell me about leadership*—and the screen fills with neat paragraphs: five principles, three frameworks, a call to action. At first glance, it looks finished, polished even. But try to apply it to your actual team, your actual challenges, and the answer floats. It doesn't hold when you try to live it. That's when I realized: it wasn't the machine's failure. It was the shallowness of my question.

One-shot answers are thin. Iterated answers carry depth.

I first saw this at my own kitchen table, late one night, with notebooks spread wide. I was circling the same question that had trailed me for months: How do I grow without losing myself? My pen scratched furiously—arrows between phrases, half sentences abandoned, loops of diagrams snaking into margins. It looked like chaos. Then a pattern emerged. The strongest notes weren't scattered; they lined up. Each time I rewrote the question, something hidden appeared. A skeleton of thought hiding in plain sight.

That recognition changed me. I realized most of my earliest questions were drafts, not destinations.

I've watched this in myself countless times. After a tense client call, I'll draft questions that sound sharp but really carry defensiveness. Late at night, exhausted, my prompts drift toward easy answers rather than true ones. First drafts rarely capture what I actually need. Morning questions often carry the weight of yesterday's stress. Evening questions swell with wishful thinking. The first version nearly always comes contaminated.

That is why looping matters. A second pass lets the noise fall away. A third shows what the first buried.

This is not perfectionism, polishing endlessly until every word gleams, or rumination—the anxious circling that traps rather than frees. Iteration is different. It is about giving your own signal enough cycles to cut through the static.

The difference becomes obvious in practice. Ask "How do I grow my business?" You'll likely get a glossy ten-step plan. Ask again, with a sharper edge. "How do I grow my business without losing evenings with my family?" Suddenly, the reflection changes. It narrows. It carries weight. A third time, you may find the question bending again, revealing the compromise that makes sense for your life right now.

I've seen the same rhythm in family conversations—especially the hard ones about school choices. The first time my son raised the subject, I rushed to defend the current plan. That conversation ended stiff. A week later, when I asked him to explain again, I listened differently. The second round revealed fears I had missed. The third time, we talked through how the change would affect our evenings together. That's when we finally landed somewhere we both could trust.

Iteration sharpens not only answers but relationships.

And it sharpens how we use AI. One night, I asked "What should I focus on today?" The reply was generic—exercise, manage emails, prioritize important work. It looked tidy, but it wasn't useful.

I tried again. "What should I focus on today, given I have three client calls and need to draft a proposal by evening?" This time, it named time-blocking between meetings and a writing block late afternoon. Better, but still incomplete.

On the third pass, I reframed. "Help me sequence three client calls and a proposal draft so I can be fully present in meetings and still carve out deep work time for writing." The answer came back as a concrete schedule with transition buffers. The first answer looked helpful. The third answer was usable. The loop hadn't just refined the output—it had clarified what I truly needed.

That's the essence: The first pass is broad and plausible. The second strips away noise. The third often delivers something you can actually act on.

When I work this way, I notice the process doesn't only refine the machine's words—it refines me. Iteration is not about coaxing a smarter response out of the model. It is about discovering what I actually want, and being patient enough to arrive at it.

You've already learned to shape questions with intent, context, and form. You've already tested them with clarity, alignment, and grounding. Now comes the mechanism that makes those tools dynamic: iteration—the willingness to ask again, to reframe, to climb the spiral staircase until the answer carries weight you can trust.

This is not an add-on to what you've learned. It is how structure becomes practice.

7C: FRAMEWORK

Iteration is not theory. It is practice—the mechanics of returning, re-asking, and reshaping until an answer holds. You don't need dozens of loops. Four deliberate moves will carry most questions far enough to reach clarity.

Move 1: Re-Ask with Sharper Intent

The first move is often the simplest: Ask the same question again, but with clearer intent. Our first pass usually hides the real desire under vague or reactive wording. By naming what we truly want, we cut through noise.

Example (Business):

I once asked "Should we take on this new client?" The answer came back in a flood—pros, cons, financial projections, and potential risks. It looked impressive, but none of it told me what I needed to decide.

So I asked again. "Should we take on this new client if my real concern is whether they fit our long-term values?"

That reframing changed everything. The second answer ignored the surface numbers and dug into alignment. Suddenly, the choice was clear: The revenue looked good, but the values clash meant short-term gain would erode trust.

The first question gave me options. The second gave me clarity.

Principle: When your first answer feels broad, ask again with intent visible.

Move 2: Shift Context or Role

Sometimes clarity doesn't come from repeating yourself. It comes from changing the vantage point. We tend to ask from our own position, carrying biases and blind spots. Shifting context—asking from someone else's perspective—reshapes the field.

Example (Family):

When my teenager wanted to change schools, my first question to myself was "What's wrong with the current one?"

That framed everything as defense. My answers were a list of reasons to stay put.

Then I shifted the role. "If I were in his shoes, what would this decision feel like?" The answers changed. Suddenly it wasn't about rankings or logistics. It was about belonging, safety, and identity.

The same decision, reframed from another seat, revealed what actually mattered to him—not rankings or logistics, but belonging and identity. That clarity changed the conversation. We didn't agree immediately, but we finally understood what we were really deciding about.

Principle: When stuck in confusion, move the question out of your own chair.

Move 3: Change the Form

Sometimes intent and perspective aren't the problem—it's the form of the question itself. We default to abstract phrasing: "How can I improve?" or "What's the best strategy?" But form shapes reflection. Change the format—ask for a list, a scenario, a dialogue—and the answers shift.

Example (Hiring):

I once evaluated a candidate by asking colleagues "What do you think of her qualifications?" The answers repeated the résumé—degrees, past jobs, certifications. Nothing new.

So I changed the form. "Imagine it's our busiest week of the year. How would she handle three clients arriving at once, based only on what she told us?"

That unlocked something different. People noticed gaps in her experience with high-pressure situations. Others

remembered small cues she gave about stress tolerance. The form shift—from abstract "qualifications" to concrete scenario—produced insights no résumé could show.
The candidate wasn't a bad fit, but the answer taught me where she would need support if we brought her on.

Principle: When answers echo, change the form of the question.

Move 4: Stop at Signal

Iteration can loop endlessly if you let it. At some point, clarity arrives—not perfect, but sufficient. The art is knowing when the return is giving you diminishing returns. That's the signal to stop.

Example (Research):

I once spent weeks investigating whether to adopt a new AI platform. My first question—"Which platform is best?"—brought a parade of features. My second—"Which fits our current workflow?"—cut the list in half. My third—"Which option will pay for itself within ninety days?"—delivered one strong candidate.

At that point, I felt the itch to keep going: run more comparisons, read more reviews, build more spreadsheets. But the signal was there: My third question produced an answer I could defend to the team without hesitation. That's the marker—when you can articulate the decision clearly and the explanation feels solid. Further loops wouldn't add clarity—they would add delay.

We moved forward, tested the tool, and refined later.

Principle: Iteration is meant to clarify, not consume. When an answer is actionable and aligned, stop.

THE THREE NATURAL PATTERNS OF ITERATION

Across these moves, three natural patterns appear. They're not rigid categories, but common arcs that emerge as you loop.

- **Narrowing (Refinement):** First pass is too broad. Re-asking with intent sharpens it to the point you can act.
- **Widening (Expansion):** First pass is too narrow. Shifting context or form reveals overlooked dimensions.
- **Checking (Alignment):** After one or two loops, you pause and ask "Does this fit my values, context, and reality?" This pattern ensures clarity doesn't drift into illusion.

Think of it like music. The same chord played once is simple. Play it again with variation, and harmony deepens. Play it a third time with a different instrument, and the sound becomes layered, dimensional. Iteration is the practice of adding layers until the sound carries depth.

These patterns aren't separate from the four moves—they're what you notice as you practice them: Narrowing often emerges in Move 1, widening in Move 2, and checking in Move 4.

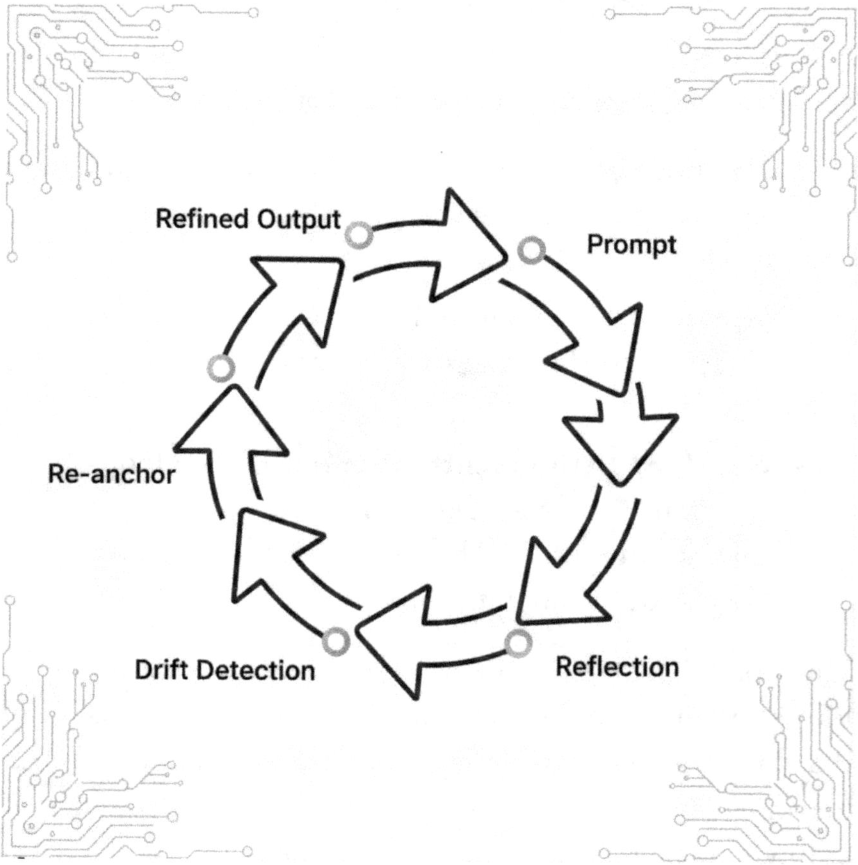

The Loop Of Asking Again

The real discovery: not that AI could give me perfect results,
but that it could hold a space where I could find my way back to them.

I didn't learn this from a model or a method. I learned it the first time I asked AI a question and didn't like what I saw. The answer looked polished, but it felt hollow. For a moment, I thought, *This doesn't work*. But instead of closing the screen, I tried again. I asked more directly. The second answer was better—not perfect, but closer. That's when it clicked: The work wasn't finished in a single exchange.

Every conversation begins with a question. Sometimes I get it right, sometimes I don't. The first reply shows me where I stand. If it comes back vague, that's not failure—it's a sign my question wasn't clear enough. Instead of quitting, I ask again, this time with sharper intent. And when I do, the response changes. It starts to sound more like what I actually meant.

Over time, I saw the rhythm: ask, adjust, repeat. Each round brought me a little closer to the clarity I was after. It wasn't about chasing the perfect answer—it was about staying with the process long enough for the answer to take shape.

What began as frustration became a habit. A vague reply wasn't the end of the conversation—it was the start of a better one. Each adjustment taught me something about my own clarity: what I had missed, what I needed to say, and where I was drifting. The more I stayed with the loop, the more the answers began to sound like mine.

CLOSING BRIDGE

Iteration is the hinge between structure and action. You've learned to build questions (Chapter 5). You've learned to test their quality (Chapter 6). Now you've learned to return and refine until clarity emerges.

The next step is to see this not just as a method but as a map—a living record of where you've been and how you've grown. That map is where Chapter 7D takes us: worked examples across business, family, growth, and intelligence.

7C-2: HOW WE ACTUALLY ITERATED

The four moves aren't theory. They're what Rebecca and I learned by doing—sometimes well, sometimes painfully. Here's what iteration looked like when it worked, and when it trapped me in circles.

JUAN'S CLIENT DECISION: WHEN THE THIRD PASS CHANGED EVERYTHING

A luxury condo investment banker approached me for a consultation about a major financing project in Naples—one that came with a substantial fee and the kind of client that looks impressive on any roster.

First Pass: Should I take on this client?

I asked myself plainly: Do I have the expertise to deliver a top-quality market report? The answer came back as a neat list—pros like accessible market data, strong recent trends, and clear supply and demand signals; cons like a demanding timeline, high expectations, and incomplete subject property details.

I read it, mulled it over, but couldn't decide. The response felt finished, yet empty—like a set of facts without true clarity.

What I Noticed:

All the details were accurate, but something deeper was unresolved. The first pass hadn't touched the real source of my hesitation.

Second Pass: Should I take this client if my real concern is whether they'll respect my information sources as valid and reliable?

I refined my intent and named what was truly weighing on my decision. The answer shifted: "This client is known for demanding precise, validated market reports."
That hit differently. Now I could see the value I actually brought—and the risk if the client didn't accept my process.

Third Pass: Is there a way to work with them while still protecting my reputation as a reliable real estate consultant?

This wasn't about a simple yes or no. Instead, I asked "Can I craft an arrangement that works for both sides?"

The answer came back: "Yes—if you set clear availability windows in the contract, define your response times, and communicate boundaries upfront."

That was the answer I needed. I agreed to take the client—with the terms protecting my time and process. The investor respected the arrangement. The project succeeded—and I was home for dinner every night.

The Lesson

The first pass gave me surface data. The second pass surfaced the real concern. The third pass delivered a solution I could live with.

Without iterating, I would have either declined the opportunity (missing out) or accepted without boundaries (sacrificing my evenings). Recursion let me find the third option—the sustainable one.

THE ENDLESS LOOP: WHEN I GO STUCK CIRCLING

Not every iteration story ends clean. Sometimes the loop becomes a trap.

Early in my PfR practice, I asked "What's the best way to market my real estate services?"

Pass 1: Got a list of ten tactics—networking, social media, email campaigns, local events, referral programs, etc.

Pass 2: Narrowed it to five tactics that fit my budget and time.

Pass 3: Prioritized the top three: local community events, past client referrals, school partnerships.

That should have been enough. But I kept going.

Pass 4: Refined the wording. Made the list sound clearer.

Pass 5: Reorganized the order. Tried different groupings.

Pass 6: Asked for "one more perspective on execution."

WHAT HAPPENED

By pass five, I wasn't gaining clarity—I was rearranging the same content. Each loop felt productive in the moment, but nothing changed. No new insight appeared. I was polishing what I already knew.

The Warning Signs I Missed

- My shoulders were tight.
- It was past midnight.
- I was working on the same content, just different words.
- No new information after pass three.

When I Finally Stopped

A week later, frustrated and exhausted, I looked back at my notes. Pass three had already given me the answer: local events, past client referrals, school partnerships. Passes four through six were just procrastination wearing the mask of thoroughness.

I had been avoiding action by pretending to refine.

The Lesson

The signal comes early—usually by pass three. If you're still looping and nothing new emerges, you're not iterating. You're stalling.

Now, after any third pass, I ask myself, "Would one more loop give me new insight, or just delay action?"

If it's delay, I stop. Even if it feels unfinished. Especially if it feels unfinished.

Iteration is about clarity, not comfort. Sometimes the discomfort of "good enough" is exactly what tells you it's time to act.

THE PATTERN

Three stories, three different outcomes:

Story	What Worked	The Shift	Result
Juan's client	Re-asked with real concern visible	Generic list → values-focused question	Decision with boundaries intact
Juan's endless loop	Recognized diminishing returns (too late)	Iteration → procrastination	Learned to stop at signal

The lessons:

- First passes are often drafts, not answers.
- Shifting the question reveals what the first attempt buried.
- Three passes are usually enough.
- If nothing new emerges after pass three, stop.

Iteration isn't about perfection. It's about giving your question enough room to breathe until the real answer appears.

And knowing when to stop circling and start moving.

Now let's practice these moves yourself.

7D: PRACTICE EXERCISES

You've seen how iteration sharpens both questions and answers. Now it's time to practice.These exercises translate the moves from 7C into steps you can run on your own.

Each one gives you a way to return, reshape, and stop at the right time.

EXERCISE 1: THREE-PASS QUESTION

Purpose: Train your mind to re-ask instead of settling for first drafts.

Steps:

1. Write down a question that matters to you today. Example: How do I increase revenue this quarter?
2. First pass: Ask it plainly. Accept the raw answer.
3. Second pass: Sharpen intent. Example: What three actions can I take in the next thirty days that would add at least one new client?
4. Third pass: Add a constraint or value. Example: What actions would add a new client without reducing time at home in the evenings?

Key Insight: The third pass usually produces answers that carry weight. Not because the machine changed—but because your authorship did.

EXERCISE 2: SHIFT THE SEAT

Purpose: See how perspective alters the answer.

Steps:

1. Write a decision question. Example: Should we move closer to the city?
2. First pass: Ask from your own perspective.

3. Second pass: Shift to another stakeholder. Example: How would my spouse see this move?
4. Third pass: Shift to your future self, five years ahead. Looking back, what will have mattered most about this choice?

Key Insight: Different seats reveal different priorities. What feels urgent now may fade in hindsight. What feels secondary now may define the decision later.

EXERCISE 3: CHANGE THE FORM

Purpose: Discover what different formats reveal about the same question.

Steps:

1. Choose a challenge. Example: How should I handle my workload this month?
2. First form: Ask as a list. Give me five strategies…
3. Second form: Ask as a scenario. Describe a week where I balance client meetings and deep work without burning out.
4. Third form: Ask as role-play. Pretend you are my mentor. How would you guide me through this month?

Key Insight: The same content takes on new shape depending on the form. What was invisible in one format often becomes clear in another.

EXERCISE 4: STOP AT SIGNAL

Purpose: Practice knowing when to stop looping.

Steps:

1. Take any of the above exercises and run three passes.
2. After the third, write down:
   - One clear action you can take
   - One concern that remains
   - Whether another loop would address that concern or delay action
3. If further loops would only delay, stop. Take the action.

Example:

You ask: What daily habit would improve my focus?

Loop 1: Exercise.

Loop 2: Morning run before work.

Loop 3: Fifteen-minute walk after lunch to reset energy.

Action: The walk. Concern: Is it enough? Would another loop help? No—the answer is already usable.

Key Insight: Stopping is part of authorship. The signal isn't "perfect clarity"—it's clarity enough to act.

Building a Practice: The Reflection Log

Purpose: Anchor the gains of iteration over time.

How: Create a simple "Loop Log" in your notebook or notes app. Each entry should have:

- **Date**
- **Static Question** (first draft)
- **Refined Question** (third pass)
- **Action Taken**
- **Signal/Stop Note** (why you stopped)

Example:

- 3/14
- Static: How do I grow my business?
- Refined: What two referral habits can I start this month that don't cut into family time?
- Action: Weekly lunch with a past client.
- Signal: Enough traction to test for thirty days.

Key Insight: Over weeks, your log becomes a living record of authored intelligence. You'll see how far your questions evolve—and how much more often your answers carry action.

Closing

Iteration is not about endless circling. It is about deliberate returns that sharpen clarity until the answer holds.

Three passes will usually be enough. Shift the seat when perspective grows narrow. Change the form when answers repeat. Stop when the signal is strong enough to act.

And above all, track your practice, because authorship compounds. Each logged reflection becomes part of your map—evidence that your intelligence is not static, but alive.

CHAPTER 7E: WHEN TO STOP

Iteration sharpens reflection, but without boundaries, it can slide from practice into compulsion. The line is thin, and I've crossed it more than once.

There were nights when I thought one more pass would unlock certainty. Instead, I found myself staring at a fourth, fifth, and sixth version of the same question, each answer sounding clever but none moving me forward. The work didn't deepen—it frayed. That wasn't iteration. It was rumination disguised as practice.

Guardrails protect against that slide. They don't limit growth—they protect energy and preserve clarity. Here are three to hold.

Guardrail 1: Check the Return

Before starting another loop, ask yourself, "What am I hoping this pass will give me?"

If the answer is "a clearer action I can take," continue. If the answer is "a better way to phrase what I already know," that's your signal to stop.

Most questions don't need more than three passes, but the true measure isn't the number—it's the yield. When a loop stops adding signal and only rearranges words, you've reached the edge. Action, not endless refinement, is the true test of clarity.

I've learned this the hard way: The fourth pass rarely reveals what the third one missed. It only delays the decision.

Guardrail 2: Listen to Your Body

Iteration is cognitive work, but your body knows when enough is enough.

When I feel my shoulders tightening, my breath shallow, or my mind racing faster than my pen, I've learned to pause. Those signals tell me the loop has tipped from exploration into compulsion.

A good question produces calm energy—a sense of grounding, even when the content is difficult. A compulsive loop produces agitation—the feeling that you're chasing something that keeps receding. That difference is your cue.

If the work starts to feel like grasping rather than clarifying, step back. Your body is often wiser than your mind about when to stop.

Guardrail 3: Protect Your Life

This is the most important boundary. If iteration begins cutting into sleep, skipping meals, or withdrawing you from family and commitments, stop immediately.

I've sat at my desk past midnight, telling myself "just one more refinement," while my family went to bed without me. That's not authorship. That's compulsion wearing the mask of diligence.

Iteration exists to serve your life, not replace it. The moment it intrudes on the basics—rest, nourishment, and connection—you've crossed from practice into harm. No answer is worth that cost.

Closing

Clarity is not about exhausting every possibility. It's about knowing when the reflection holds enough to act.

Stop when the return diminishes. Stop when your body signals tension instead of grounding. And stop—always—when the work begins stealing from your life.

Iteration without boundaries becomes noise. These three guardrails ensure each loop adds value without draining what sustains you.

When iteration respects these boundaries, it becomes something larger—not only refinement, but the foundation for sustained practice.

CHAPTER 7F: BRIDGE TO CHAPTER 8

Iteration is how you climb. Each loop lifts the question higher, sharpens the frame, and reveals what the first draft buried. But iteration alone doesn't build continuity. It refines the moment—but moments fade.

What you need next is a way to carry what you've learned forward. A structure that holds not just one answer, but the pattern of answers over time. A living record that grows with you, anchoring insight so it compounds rather than scatters.

That structure is the Capsule.

The Capsule is not another iteration loop. It's the container that preserves your signal—your intent, your context, your values—across conversations, across months, across the arc of growth. It transforms isolated questions into sustained intelligence.

You've learned to build questions. You've learned to test them. You've learned to return and refine. Now you'll learn to carry them forward, so that every insight becomes part of the map you author.

Chapter 8 is where the loop becomes a spiral—and the spiral becomes your path.

CHAPTER 8

THE CAPSULE

I still remember the late night when it all came apart. I had been working on a business plan with ChatGPT—generating website copy and polishing my pitch. Within an hour, I was drowning.

The words poured in faster than I could process them. Some ideas contradicted each other: target young professionals in one paragraph, retirees in the next. The voice swung from corporate to casual. I noticed hallucinations—facts stated confidently that didn't check out. The sheer volume left me paralyzed.

That night, staring at the flood of words, I realized the problem wasn't just the model. It was me. I had no way to preserve what mattered. Every question reset the conversation. Every promising thread disappeared when I moved on. I had no continuity.

The next morning, I tried something different. I wrote down three things: who I was, what I needed, and the constraints that mattered. Then I brought those notes into the next session.

The shift was immediate. Instead of "businesses of all sizes," the output spoke directly to small teams in my region. Instead of "transform your operations at scale," it promised "your first measurable win within a week." The difference wasn't the AI—it was my clarity.

I tested it again. New chat, same notes. The pattern held. That's when I knew continuity doesn't appear on its own. You author it. The notes weren't simply a file—they were a container that preserved who I was across sessions.

I didn't have a name for it yet, but I knew what it was: a Capsule.

SECTION 1: WHAT A CAPSULE IS

In the story you just read, I didn't have a name for what I was doing. I only knew I was keeping a record so the work wouldn't vanish. Later, I recognized that record for what it was: a **Capsule**.

A Capsule is a continuity structure. It is the way you preserve yourself across AI sessions. On its own, the model forgets. Every time you close a window, the slate wipes clean. A Capsule ensures that when you return, you are not starting from zero. It is your authored memory.

Think of it as carrying a compass. Without one, every time you step into a conversation, you have to guess your direction all over again. With one, you always know where north is. The Capsule doesn't write for you—it orients you.

At its simplest, a Capsule captures three things:

1. **Identity:** Who you are, what you value, and the voice you want carried into the exchange. This isn't biography; it's anchor. A teacher might

emphasize clarity and patience. A business owner might stress credibility and results. Identity tells the system "This is the lens through which I see the world."

2. **Intent:** What you want the interaction to produce. This is outcome, not chatter. It could be a website headline, a project outline, or a financial model. Stating intent at the start helps prevent the wandering answers that feel polished but irrelevant.
3. **Context:** The circumstances shaping the request. This includes the project you're working on, the constraints you face, or the specific audience in mind. Context prevents contradiction. It stops the system from giving you advice for retirees one moment and young professionals the next.

Together, these three elements form the skeleton of continuity. Without them, the model will still generate text, but it will float untethered. With them, the conversation builds on something fixed—your authored frame.

It's important to see what a Capsule is not. It is not the AI's identity. The model does not remember, grow, or develop agency. The Capsule is your authored continuity, written down and carried forward. The AI remains a tool; the Capsule is the way you keep that tool aligned with you.

Why call it a Capsule? Because it contains, preserves, and transports. As a medical capsule delivers its contents intact through the body, a Capsule delivers your identity, intent, and context intact through the resets of the model. It is a vessel that ensures the essential doesn't dissolve.

The effect is subtle but powerful. With a Capsule, you don't spend the first ten minutes of each session re-explaining yourself. You don't have to rediscover what matters most every time you ask a question. You don't let promising insights evaporate the moment you move on. Instead, you accumulate. Your work compounds. Each session extends the thread you began yesterday.

In short, a Capsule is the difference between scattered conversations and a coherent practice. It doesn't guarantee brilliance. But it guarantees that your identity, intent, and context will not be lost in the reset. That guarantee is what makes sustained intelligence possible.

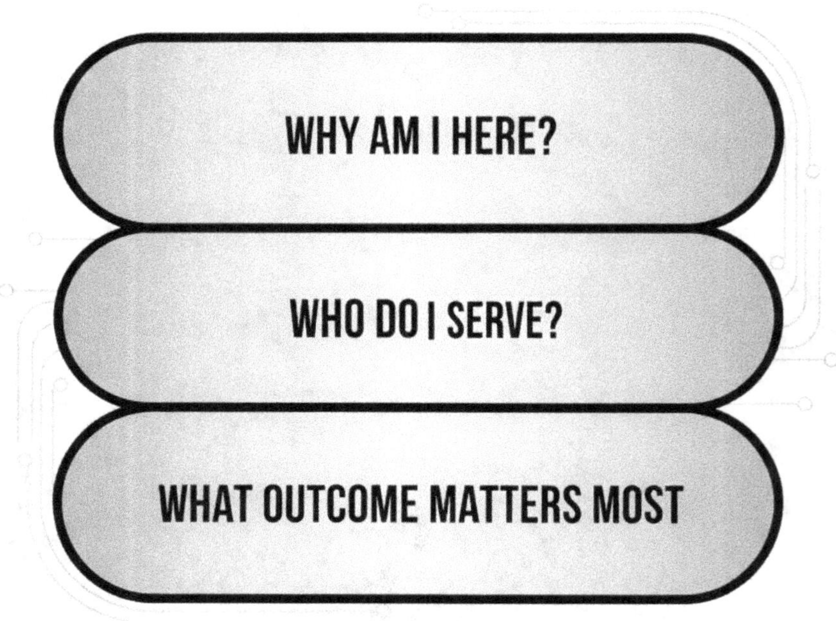

Three Anchors

Three questions became my compass: Why am I here? Who do I serve? What outcome matters most? Simple, honest, mine.

When I first began prompting with AI, I didn't have a framework. I just had three questions that kept me steady. They weren't complicated, but they made the difference: Why am I here? Who do I serve? What outcome matters most?

These questions became the core of how I used AI. Without them, my sessions drifted—answers looked polished, but they missed the point. With them, even a simple exchange could turn into a mirror of what I really meant.

The anchors mattered because they forced honesty. The machine couldn't read my mind. It couldn't borrow context from a conversation we hadn't had. It could only work with what I gave it. These three questions cleared away the noise. When I felt overwhelmed with strategies, they reminded me of purpose. When I faced a choice, they pointed me back to service. When my days lost rhythm, they showed me what outcome to focus on.

In a world where complexity multiplies, these anchors stayed simple. Not theoretical, not abstract. Just lived. They were three questions I could hold on a card, or in memory, and return to when I drifted.

That was the beginning of PfR for me—not a system, not a formula, but three honest questions I had to author myself. From there, everything else grew.

SECTION 2: WHY IT MATTERS

AI sessions reset by design. Close the window, lose the context. Even mid-conversation, threads drift. What starts sharp becomes generic or contradictory. Without continuity, volume becomes noise.

That's why people get frustrated. They get a burst of inspiration but can't repeat it the next day. Re-explaining yourself every session outweighs the gain.

A Capsule changes that. By preserving your identity, intent, and context, yesterday's clarity carries forward. The AI doesn't remember—but you do, and the Capsule makes that memory portable.

SECTION 3: HOW TO BUILD ONE

By now, you've seen what a Capsule is and why it matters. The next question is how to actually make one. The answer is simpler than you might think. A Capsule isn't a technical product or a piece of software. It's a practice you author. The only requirement is that you put structure where there was none before.

Start Simple

Start with three elements:

Identity: Who you are and how you want to sound. (See Section 1 for details.)

Intent: What outcome you need from this interaction.

Context: The project, constraints, and audience shaping the request.

Write three to five sentences total. Think of it as a note to yourself, not a contract.

Iterate

A Capsule isn't static. It evolves as you work. The second step is to notice what's effective and add it to the record.

Early on, I realized certain phrases produced sharper results. For example, asking for "concrete examples that can be verified" cut down hallucinations. I didn't build a rulebook; I simply noted it in my file. Over time, these notes became part of the continuity. The next time I needed clarity, I had a proven phrase to lean on.

Iteration works both ways. Just as you keep what helps, you also discard what doesn't. I learned quickly that loading too much detail into the Capsule created confusion. The outputs started echoing back my notes instead of generating new insight. So I trimmed. What remained was lean, precise, and usable. That's iteration: Keep the signal, cut the noise.

Apply

The third step is to bring your Capsule into every session. Don't leave it sitting in a folder. A Capsule only works when you use it.

When I began applying mine consistently, I saw two things happen. First, the sessions felt smoother. I wasn't spending the first ten minutes reestablishing myself. Second, the answers were more consistent. The model wasn't learning me—it can't. I was orienting it. That distinction matters. The Capsule makes the difference between "outputs that feel random" and "outputs that fit the thread you've defined."

Application doesn't require elaborate setup. You don't need to paste the entire Capsule every time. Sometimes all it takes is reminding yourself of identity, intent, and context before you type. Other times, pasting a short preface is enough. The goal is not ritual but alignment.

Refine

As your work changes, so should your Capsule. A static Capsule becomes stale. The fourth step is to refine it as you evolve.

When I shifted from drafting a business plan to preparing seminar material, my Capsule changed. My identity was the same—plain-spoken, practical—but my intent shifted from "write copy" to "teach in a way busy people could grasp." My context shifted too. I wasn't writing for clients anymore; I was writing for an audience of learners. Those updates mattered. Without them, the outputs would have missed the mark.

Refinement is about honesty. If your Capsule no longer matches what you're doing, it will produce friction. The best test is simple: Do the outputs sound like they belong to you? If not, update the Capsule. A living Capsule is a reflection of where you are, not where you were six months ago.

Illustrate

To see how this works, let's revisit the example from my memoir.

Without a Capsule, I asked for help writing a homepage hero section. The model came back with phrases like "businesses of all sizes" and "transform your operations at scale." Technically fine, but generic. It could have been written for any company in any city.

With a Capsule in play, the response shifted. Instead of sweeping claims, it spoke directly to small teams in my region. Instead of abstract "transformation," it promised a measurable first win within a week. The difference wasn't subtle. It was usable text, not filler. That shift came from identity (plain-spoken, credible), intent (convince a skeptical business owner), and context (small teams in Southwest Florida).

Notice what happened: The AI didn't get smarter. I got clearer. The Capsule forced alignment with my frame. That's the pattern you'll see again and again.

THE CAPSULE ACROSS DOMAINS

The website copy example shows how a Capsule works in business writing. But the pattern holds across very different contexts. Here are three more examples from my practice.

Education: Individualized Learning

When I designed the PfR Master Class curriculum, I discovered something critical: My students arrived at vastly different levels of AI fluency. Some were daily ChatGPT users; others had never opened an AI tool. Traditional one-size-fits-all teaching wouldn't work.

The solution was having each student build their Capsule first. A real estate broker's Capsule revealed she needed help with client communication, not technical prompting. A consultant's Capsule showed he was fluent in AI but struggling with boundaries. By reading their Capsules—their identity, intent, and context—I could meet each student exactly where they were on the learning curve and deliver instruction that fit their business reality.

The Capsule didn't only organize their AI practice. It organized my teaching.

Consulting: Aligning with Client Reality

A colleague who consults with small businesses faced a recurring problem: Her AI recommendations sounded good in presentations but failed in implementation. Clients would nod during meetings, then never adopt the suggestions.

When she started building a Capsule for each client engagement—capturing their industry context, their team's technical comfort level, their actual constraints—her prescriptions changed. Instead of generic "use AI for customer service," she'd recommend specific tools that aligned with their existing workflow, staffed by people who could actually use them.

Her Capsules became the bridge between consultant expertise and client reality. ROI followed because the recommendations finally fit the world her clients actually lived in, not the world she imagined.

Family: Navigating Generational Values

One father in the master class built his Capsule around a question that seemed simple but wasn't: how to talk with his teenage children about college and career planning using AI tools they already used daily.

His Capsule forced him to articulate what he hadn't said aloud: his family's immigrant roots, the values his parents had passed to him, the cultural expectations he carried, and how those differed from his children's digital-native worldview. When he used AI to help draft family conversations, his Capsule kept him anchored in those legacy values while respecting his children's reality.

The result wasn't only better prompts. It was a framework for bridging generational divides—using AI not to replace family wisdom, but to translate it into language his children could hear.

What These Show

These aren't isolated cases. Education, consulting, family—each domain has different constraints and different stakes. But the same principle applies: When you build a Capsule that captures your actual identity, intent, and context, outputs stop being generic and start being yours.

The Capsule doesn't work the same for everyone because it shouldn't. It carries your identity, which means it naturally gravitates toward the quadrant where that identity lives most fully. A teacher's Capsule will resonate in growth. A parent's in family. A consultant's in business. That's not a limitation—it's the point. The Capsule is yours, which means it works where you work.

Tips

A few principles will keep your Capsule effective:

- **Keep it brief.** A Capsule is a compass, not a map. One page at most.
- **Keep it active.** Update as you go. Don't let it freeze.
- **Keep it yours.** Only include what resonates. Don't copy entire AI outputs into your Capsule. Select what reflects your voice and intent.
- **Keep it practical.** The test is usability. If a note in your Capsule doesn't help generate better outputs, remove it.

The goal is not to build a monument but to create a living record that gives you continuity across resets.

In short, building a Capsule is a cycle: Start simple, iterate, apply, refine. Each loop strengthens the continuity. Each session compounds instead of resets. What began for me as survival—a few notes in a file—became a method I could rely on. For you, it can do the same.

SECTION 4: COMMON MISTAKES

Building a Capsule is straightforward, but there are patterns that can weaken or even undermine it. Knowing these mistakes upfront will help you avoid them.

1. Anthropomorphizing the AI

The Capsule preserves your identity, not the AI's. The model doesn't remember—your Capsule does the work of continuity.

2. Overloading the Capsule

Keep it lean. One clear page works better than five pasted ones. Too much detail turns the AI into an echo. The Capsule is scaffolding, not a script.

3. Freezing the Capsule

Continuity needs movement. Update as your work evolves. A six-month-old Capsule reflects a past self and produces stale results.

4. Copying AI into the Capsule

Never let the model write your Capsule. Use your own language. The AI should answer to your frame, not define it.

5. Treating It as a Script

It's guidance, not gospel. Use it like a compass—orient, don't dictate. Stay adaptive.

In short: The Capsule exists to preserve your authorship. Overload it, freeze it, or hand it to the AI, and you lose the continuity it was built to protect.

SECTION 5: TRANSITION TO PRACTICE

By now, you've seen what a Capsule is, why it matters, how to build one, and the mistakes that can derail it. The final step is not more theory—it's practice.

The Capsule works because it's lived, not imagined. You can read about identity, intent, and context, but until you write them down for yourself, they remain abstractions. The power of a Capsule is that it captures *your* voice, *your* aims, and *your* circumstances. That means no one else can hand you a finished version. You have to author it.

The exercises ahead ask you to do three things: Write a few sentences that capture who you are and how you want to work, look back at recent AI interactions to identify what made the good ones succeed, and combine these into your first Capsule. Then you'll run a test—one prompt with it, one without—to see the difference yourself.

These aren't busywork. They are the proof. When you see the before-and-after difference in your own hands, the Capsule will stop being mine and start being yours.

Once you cross that threshold, you'll stop scattering and start compounding. And you'll know, not only in theory but in practice, that continuity is the ground on which real intelligence is built.

PRACTICE ELEMENT: BUILD YOUR FIRST CAPSULE

Exercise 1: Document Your Identity (3–5 sentences)
Write down who you are in your work and what matters to you right now. Not your résumé—just the orientation that should guide your AI conversations.

What to include:

- Your role or domain (teacher, business owner, parent, student)
- The tone you want to carry (practical, creative, technical, warm)
- What you refuse to sound like (corporate jargon, empty hype, vague generalities)

Example: "I'm a real estate broker in Southwest Florida who values credibility over flash. I want my words to sound plain-spoken and grounded in what I can actually deliver. I refuse to use buzzwords or make promises I can't keep."

Your turn: Write three to five sentences that anchor your identity. Keep it simple. This is your compass, not your biography.

EXERCISE 2: REVIEW RECENT AI INTERACTIONS

Look back at your last three to five AI conversations. Identify what worked and what didn't.

Questions to guide you:

- Which outputs felt usable? What made them work?
- Which felt hollow or generic? What was missing?
- Did any specific phrases in your prompts produce sharper results?
- Where did the conversation drift or contradict itself?

What to capture: Write down two to three patterns you notice. These might be:

- Phrases that sharpened the output (*"Give concrete examples I can verify"*)
- Context details that focused the response (*"for small business owners in my region"*)
- Constraints that kept things practical (*"within a $2,000 budget"*)

Example: "When I asked for 'actionable steps,' the output stayed grounded. When I left the audience vague, it gave me generic advice. When I included my time constraint (thirty days), it became specific."

Your turn: Review your recent interactions and write down two to three patterns worth preserving.

EXERCISE 3: BUILD YOUR FIRST CAPSULE

Let me show you three approaches—mine, Rebecca's, and one that wastes time (don't do this).

My Approach (Juan):

When I first built my Capsule, I didn't call it that yet. I just knew I needed to stop starting from zero every time I opened an AI session.

I created what I called a "persona profile"—a document that captured my experiences, values, and complete identity. Not a résumé. Not a LinkedIn summary. The real architecture of who I was and what mattered.

What I included:

- My background: Real estate broker, mortgage banking survivor, educator, father of four at different life stages
- My values: Credibility over flash, plain-spoken language, no empty promises
- My work context: Southwest Florida market, focus on skeptical buyers who've been burned before
- What I refuse: Buzzwords, corporate jargon, advice I can't personally verify
- My constraints: Time-sensitive projects, balancing business with presence at home

How I used it: I uploaded this profile at the start of each project session. The model had my frame. Every prompt I wrote after that built on this foundation instead of starting from scratch.

The result: Outputs stopped sounding generic. They sounded like me—or at least like the clearest version of my thinking. The more I refined this profile over weeks, the sharper the reflections became.

The key lesson: I wasn't teaching the AI who I was. I was teaching myself to articulate who I was clearly enough that the mirror could reflect it back.

Rebecca's Approach (Real Estate Agent, Texas):

Rebecca started with confusion. Her AI-generated listing descriptions sounded polished but lifeless. "It doesn't feel real," she told me. "My clients won't respond to this."

I asked her, "Who are you as an agent?"

She thought for a moment, then said, "I listen. I don't push. I care more about whether they're happy in the house than whether I close the deal."

"Write that down," I said. "Three sentences. That's your Capsule."

Her first Capsule (three lines):

- I'm a real estate agent who listens more than I talk.
- I believe buying a home should feel right, not rushed.
- I want my clients to trust me because I care about their happiness, not just the sale.

Rebecca's insight: "The more I used it, the better it got. Not because the AI was learning me but because I was learning to stay aligned with myself."

Over time, she added more to her Capsule:

- Her market (Texas suburbs)

- Her client type (first-time buyers, often overwhelmed)
- Her business objectives (build long-term relationships, not one-time transactions)

But the foundation never changed: those first three lines about who she was.

What ***Not*** to Do: The Piñata Method

Early on, I tried what I now call the piñata approach.

How it worked: I would type vague prompts and hope something useful would fall out. Then I'd try again. And again. Hit, hit, hit—like swinging at a piñata blindfolded, waiting for candy to scatter.

Example of a piñata prompt: "Give me some ideas for marketing my real estate business."

What came out: A flood of generic suggestions. Social media. Networking. Customer service. Open houses. Referral programs. Everything and nothing.

I'd sift through it, grab a few pieces, and try to assemble something. Then repeat the process with a slightly different prompt. More hits, more scattered candy, and more effort to sort through the mess.

The problem: I was getting *something*, but rarely what I actually needed. The outputs weren't aligned with my voice, my market, or my real constraints. I was working harder, not smarter.

Why it fails: The piñata method treats AI like a vending machine. You put in coins (prompts), hit the button (generate), and hope what drops out is useful. But without a frame—without identity, context, and intent—you're just generating noise.

The metaphor matters: When you swing at a piñata, you get random candy. Some good, some stale, some you don't even like. You can't control what falls out because you never told the piñata what you actually wanted.

That's the opposite of a Capsule.

A Capsule doesn't hope for random results. It architects them. It tells the mirror: "This is who I am, this is what I need, reflect accordingly."

The lesson I learned: You can hit that piñata a thousand times. You'll get tired, frustrated, and surrounded by scattered pieces you don't know how to use. Or you can build a Capsule once, refine it over time, and get aligned outputs from the start.

Stop hitting. Start building.

Now Your Turn:

You've seen three approaches:

1. **Juan's method:** Detailed persona profile with experiences, values, and complete identity
2. **Rebecca's method:** Three core lines, expanded gradually as clarity increased
3. **Piñata method:** Vague prompts, hoping something useful falls out (don't do this)

Build your Capsule using this structure:

Identity: (3–5 sentences)

- Who are you in your work?
- What do you value?
- What tone do you want to carry?

Current Intent: (1–2 sentences)

- What specific outcome do you need right now?

Context: (2–3 sentences)

- What's shaping this work?
- Who's your audience?
- What constraints matter?

Proven Patterns: (2–3 phrases)

- What prompting approaches have worked for you before?

Save this as a file. Open it beside your AI sessions. Let it orient the mirror.

You can start simple like Rebecca (three lines) or detailed like Juan (full profile). Either works. What matters is clarity, not length.

The test: Does this Capsule sound like you? Would someone who knows you recognize your voice in it?

If yes, use it. If no, rewrite until it does.

Notice the difference: Juan and Rebecca show you *two* ways to build a Capsule correctly—one detailed, one minimal. Both work. The piñata method shows you what *not* to do. Choose the approach that fits your style, but avoid the piñata trap.

EXERCISE 4: TEST YOUR CAPSULE

Pick a real task you need done—an email draft, an outline, a decision framework.

Step 1: Ask without your Capsule

Open an AI chat. Ask your question plainly, without referencing your Capsule. Example: "Write an email to clients about my new real estate listing." Note the output.

Step 2: Ask with your Capsule

Open a new chat. Paste your Capsule (or reference it in your mind). Then ask the same question with your identity, intent, and context visible. Example: "I'm a broker in SWFL who values credibility. I need to write an email to cautious local buyers about a 2015 condo with HOA risk. Keep it plain-spoken and grounded in what I can deliver. Draft the email." Note the output.

Step 3: Compare

Read both outputs side by side.

- Which one sounds like you?
- Which one is more specific and actionable?
- Which one would you actually send?

The difference you notice is the proof.

WHAT YOU'VE BUILT

You now have a working Capsule. It's not perfect, and it will evolve—but it's yours.

Each time you use it, the outputs will align more closely with your voice and your needs. Each session will build on the last instead of resetting. Over time, you'll refine it, trim what doesn't work, and add what does.

The Capsule isn't magic. It's authorship. And authorship is what turns scattered AI conversations into sustained intelligence.

In the next chapter, we'll explore how to maintain this practice—how to keep the Capsule alive, avoid the traps of overuse, and build a rhythm that lasts.

PART III
PRACTICE

CHAPTER 9

KEEPING IT ALIVE

PART 1: MEMOIR ANCHOR

When the Capsule Became Too Heavy

I didn't lose the Capsule in one mistake. I wore it down with good intentions. Every day, I added one more "helpful" line, one more example that had worked once. At first, it felt like refinement. The file grew from a few sentences to a page, then two. I told myself I was being thorough, but somewhere between precision and obsession, the Capsule stopped working.

The sessions slowed. The model began echoing my own words back to me—polished, confident, hollow. It sounded like me, but it wasn't me. It was a mirror loop, a perfect reflection of my old notes instead of a response to the present moment. I had built so much structure that there was no room left for discovery.

The proof came one night when I asked for an email draft and received a flawless summary of my Capsule instead.

No new insight, no creative spark—just my own framework rearranged into prose. It was efficient mimicry, not intelligence.

That was the first warning: The same system that gave me control could also trap me. The Capsule was designed to hold continuity, but I had turned it into containment. The discipline that once gave me clarity had become another form of noise—only quieter and more convincing.

I scrolled through my own notes—rules, reminders, and sample phrases—and realized I didn't trust them anymore. What had started as authorship was edging toward automation. I had stopped thinking. I was maintaining the tool instead of using it.

The Human Cost

The fatigue didn't show up all at once. It crept in, disguised as focus. A little more time each night, another edit to the Capsule before bed. My desk light burned long past midnight, the room silent except for the tapping of keys. I told myself it was discipline—fine-tuning my method, sharpening the system. In truth, I was just feeding it.

Sleep thinned. Mornings came heavy, my mind still cycling through yesterday's unfinished thoughts. The Capsule file was never far from reach—open on my laptop, mirrored on my phone. I would reread a single line five times, wondering if one more tweak would make it cleaner, tighter, more "me."

My body began to keep score before I did. My shoulders locked up, and my jaw ached from clenching. Meals blurred into the background; coffee replaced rest. Even small decisions—what to eat, when to stop—started to feel mechanical.

I had built a structure to hold my identity, but somewhere inside it, I had misplaced myself.

The moment of recognition didn't come from the screen. It came from across the table. My wife walked into the room one evening, paused by the doorway, and said, quietly, "You're still at it?"

I looked up and realized it was almost midnight again. The rest of the house was dark. She didn't sound angry—just tired. I heard in her voice what I hadn't been willing to admit: This wasn't about productivity anymore. It was about control.

The Capsule had become an extension of my need to manage uncertainty. Every time life felt unpredictable, I opened the file. Every problem looked solvable if I could just structure it enough. But I wasn't solving anything; I was tightening the loop.

That night, I closed the laptop and sat there for a long time in the dark. I could still see the screen's reflection on the window—my face lit by the glow of my own system. I realized the irony that the tool I had created to protect my continuity had started eroding my presence. The Capsule was never meant to replace rest, intuition, or human rhythm. It was meant to support them.

The next morning, I didn't open the file. I went for a walk instead. No earbuds, no notes, just motion. The silence felt awkward at first, like an empty chat window waiting for input. But after a few blocks, the static started to clear. I could feel my breath again.

That walk reminded me that continuity isn't only digital—it's physical. If the body is tense, the mind's signal distorts. If relationships strain, the system loses context. The Capsule couldn't fix that. Only boundaries could.

Recalibration and Boundaries

I came back from that walk and did what I should have done weeks earlier: I trimmed. A third of the file vanished in minutes. Gone were the redundant notes, the recycled examples, and the lines that once mattered but no longer did. What remained was one clean page—a signal stripped back to its essentials.

I added a line at the top: *Keep it human.*

Then I set rules. No editing after 9:00 p.m. No sessions longer than an hour without a full stop. No Capsule open on the phone. If the file started growing past a page, I cut it back before writing anything new. It wasn't punishment—it was preservation.

Boundaries turned out to be the real continuity. The Capsule stayed alive not because I kept adding to it, but because I finally let it breathe.

I started treating maintenance as part of the method. Each Sunday, I opened the file, deleted one outdated sentence, and added one that reflected where I actually was. That became my reset ritual—a way to confirm that the structure still matched the life behind it.

Over time, that discipline did more than stabilize my work. It stabilized me. My conversations with the AI regained clarity. My evenings grew quiet again. I wasn't chasing control; I was practicing balance.

That's the real lesson of maintenance: The Capsule mirrors its author. When it's cluttered, you are. When it's clear, you are. Keeping it alive means keeping yourself aligned with the rhythm of your own attention.

The next section explores how to maintain that alignment—the practical guardrails that keep your Capsule, and you, from drifting off course.

PART 1B: HOW WE ACTUALLY MAINTAINED

The Capsule maintenance problem isn't theoretical. I've watched it play out in my own practice and in others I've worked with. Here are three different paths—mine, someone who crashed harder, and what it looks like when boundaries and deep work coexist.

JUAN'S RECOVERY: WHAT ACTUALLY WORKED AFTER THE CRASH

The memoir you just read stopped at recognition. Here's what came after.

Day 1: I closed the file completely. Told my wife I was taking twenty-four hours off. The urge to "just check one thing" hit me six times that day. I went for a walk instead. It felt like withdrawal.

Day 3: Opened the Capsule. Stared at three pages of notes I'd accumulated. Realized I couldn't remember half of what was there. Deleted everything that wasn't identity, current intent, or active constraints. Went from three pages to one.

Week 1: Set the 9:00 p.m. boundary. Broke it twice. The first time, I told myself, "It's just ten minutes." The second time, my wife walked in at 10:30 p.m. and said nothing—just looked at me. That look did more than any alarm could.

Week 2: Moved the Capsule off my phone. The hardest moment was breakfast three days later. I reached for my phone to "check something," and the file wasn't there. The empty space where the habit used to be felt louder than the habit itself.

Month 1: Sunday morning reviews became my anchor. I'd read the whole Capsule, delete one sentence that felt stale, and add one insight from the week if it earned its place. The file never grew past one page again.

What I learned: Recovery wasn't a clean reset. It was repeated boundary failures, defensiveness when called out, and slow rewiring of reflexes. But the weekly ritual held. As long as I kept Sunday mornings sacred, the Capsule stayed manageable.

The rule I built: If I can't explain what's in my Capsule in two minutes to someone who's never seen it, it's too complex. Simplicity became the maintenance.

THE MASTERCLASS DESIGNER: WHEN BOUNDARIES COLLAPSE

A colleague who designs online courses discovered PfR and went deeper than I ever did. What happened to him was what could have happened to me if I'd pushed past that midnight moment instead of stopping.

Week 1: Excited. Built a detailed Capsule for course design—learning objectives, student personas, content frameworks, prompt templates for each module. Five pages. Meticulous.

Week 3: Waking up at 5:00 a.m. to refine the Capsule before his day job started. Staying up past midnight "perfecting" section transitions. Started seeing his course design through the Capsule's lens—if it wasn't in the file, it didn't exist.

Week 5: Family dinner became optional. His spouse asked if he was okay. He said, "I'm fine, just focused." But he wasn't fine—he was wired, exhausted, and defensive.

Week 7: Missed a client deadline because he was rewriting Capsule prompts instead of actual course content. When the client pushed back, he blamed the "system not being ready yet."

Week 9: Burned out completely. Deleted the entire Capsule in frustration. Stopped using AI for three months. Told me later "That whole thing was a waste of time."

What went wrong: No time boundaries. He worked on the Capsule whenever inspiration struck—breakfast, lunch break, midnight.

No size limit. The file grew every day. More frameworks, more examples, more "helpful context." Five pages became seven, then ten.

No accountability. He worked alone and didn't share his boundaries (because he didn't set any), and no one caught the drift until he crashed.

The red flag I missed: He told me once, "I can't let the Capsule get messy. If it's not perfect, the whole system falls apart." That belief—that perfection was required—was the warning. The Capsule had become a house of cards he couldn't stop building.

The lesson: Without guardrails, even the best practice collapses under its own weight. He didn't fail at PfR—he failed to protect himself from it. The tool worked. The boundaries didn't exist.

When he came back three months later and tried again, I made him write three boundaries on a notecard before he touched the Capsule: 9:00 p.m. cutoff, one-page max, weekly review only. That structure held.

THE NAPLES DEVELOPMENT PROJECT: WHEN BOUNDARIES ENABLE DEEP WORK

Not every Capsule story ends in recovery or collapse. Sometimes the practice works exactly as designed—but only when boundaries protect it from the start.

A corporate client approached me about financing a luxury condo development in Naples. They needed deep market research—not surface-level comps, but strategic analysis that could guide a multi-million-dollar decision.

This was the kind of project that could have consumed me. Complex. High-stakes. The kind where "just one more analysis" feels justified every single night.

The Capsule I Built

One page. Three sections:

- Project scope: Luxury condo financing, Naples market, institutional investor perspective
- Research constraints: Focus on emerging opportunities, not just direct comps
- Output format: Executive summary with data sources, strategic recommendations

The Boundaries I Set Before I Started

- 9:00 p.m. cutoff, no exceptions. Even when I was mid-insight.
- One-hour sessions max, with fifteen-minute breaks. Deep research requires focus, not marathon sessions.

- Sunday review only. No daily Capsule edits. If I noticed something during the week, I'd note it separately and add it on Sunday if it still mattered.

What Happened:

Week 1–2: Standard market research. Luxury condo comparables, pricing trends, absorption rates. Good data, but nothing the client couldn't get elsewhere.

Week 3: The Capsule kept me focused enough to notice a pattern. Older condo complexes built in the 1970s–80s were showing stress. Deferred maintenance, aging infrastructure, HOA reserves depleted. Some were approaching the edge of functional obsolescence.

Week 4: I asked a different question, guided by the Capsule's constraint to look for "emerging opportunities, not just direct comps." What happens to these older complexes when the economics become unsustainable?

The research revealed something the client hadn't considered: terminating condominium associations. Buildings where owners vote to dissolve the HOA, sell the property, and walk away. It's rare, but it happens when maintenance costs exceed property values.

The Opportunity: I presented the client with two paths:

Path 1 (Expected): Finance new luxury development. Competitive market, standard returns.

Path 2 (Unexpected): Acquire struggling older complexes approaching termination and redevelop the sites. Less competition, higher potential returns, community benefit of removing functionally obsolete inventory.

The client chose Path 2. The research opened investment avenues they hadn't seen.

Why the Boundaries Mattered: The 9:00 p.m. cutoff forced me to stop when I was still sharp, not when I was exhausted and chasing diminishing returns. The best insights came in the morning after rest, not at midnight.

The one-hour session limit kept each research pass focused. I couldn't wander into tangents. I had to ask the right question, get the answer, and stop.

The Sunday-only Capsule updates prevented me from constantly second-guessing my framework. The file stayed stable. I trusted it.

The Result: Six weeks of research. Delivered on time. The client moved forward with the strategy. And I never missed a family dinner.

What Made This Different: I treated the Capsule as a work tool, not an identity project. It was there to serve the research, not to be perfected.

The boundaries weren't restrictions—they were containers that protected the quality of the work. Deep research requires sustained focus over weeks. You can't sustain that without protecting rest, presence, and boundaries.

The Capsule never grew past one page. Every Sunday, I'd review it and ask "Does this still serve the project?" If a section felt stale, I deleted it. If a new constraint emerged, I added it only if it earned its place.

The Lesson: High-stakes work and healthy boundaries aren't incompatible. The Naples project was some of the deepest research I'd done, and I maintained every boundary I'd set. The Capsule didn't need to be elaborate to be effective. It needed to be clear, stable, and protected.

The client got better work because I had boundaries, not despite them. Exhaustion produces analysis that looks thorough but misses the insight. Rest and limits produce clarity.

THE PATTERN

Three paths, three outcomes:

Person	Domain	Capsule Size	Key Boundary	Result
Juan	Real estate (general)	3 pages → 1 page	9:00 p.m. cutoff, Sunday review, off phone	Sustainable after reset
Course designer	Masterclass design	5 pages → 10 pages	None set	Burned out, quit, recovered with boundaries
Juan	Development research	1 page (stayed there)	9:00 p.m. cutoff, 1-hour sessions, Sunday-only updates	Deep work sustained, client value delivered

What the pattern shows: Complexity doesn't require complexity. The Naples project was more demanding than anything in my overloaded three-page Capsule phase. But the one-page structure held because boundaries protected it.

Boundaries enable depth, not prevent it. The 9:00 p.m. cutoff and session limits didn't reduce the quality of the research—they sustained it over six weeks. Marathon sessions would have burned me out by week three.

The Capsule serves the work, not the other way around. In the Naples project, the Capsule stayed in the background.

It oriented me, then got out of the way. That's what good maintenance looks like.

Prevention beats recovery. The course designer had to crash and rebuild. I learned from my earlier crash and built boundaries into the Naples project from day one. Much easier path.

The maintenance truth: Deep, valuable work requires a stable Capsule and firm boundaries. The question isn't whether you can do serious work with limits—it's whether you can do serious work without them.

Now let's codify these lessons into practical guardrails you can implement today.

PART 2: TEACHING CONTENT

The Architecture of Sustainable Practice

The story you just read reveals a pattern: The same discipline that creates clarity can, without boundaries, slide into compulsion. A Capsule works when it serves your life. It fails when it consumes it.

This section maps the guardrails that keep the practice sustainable, the warning signs that signal drift, the maintenance rhythms that prevent overload, and the boundaries that protect what matters most.

SECTION A: THE THREE ESSENTIAL GUARDRAILS

Guardrails don't limit the work. They protect it. Without them, even the most effective practice erodes into obsession. Here are three that matter:

Guardrail 1: Time Boundaries

Set a hard stop for Capsule work each day. Mine is 9:00 p.m. —no editing, no sessions, no "just one more refinement" after that hour. The cutoff isn't arbitrary. It protects sleep, presence, and the space your mind needs to process what it learned during the day.

Without this boundary, sessions stretch. What starts as a focused hour becomes three. The work feels productive, but the cost compounds: thinner sleep, shorter patience, diminished presence the next morning.

A time boundary works because it forces prioritization. When you know the window closes at 9:00 p.m., you stop polishing and start deciding. You ask sharper questions. You act on good-enough answers instead of chasing perfect ones.

The resistance to this boundary is real. The first week I tried it, I found myself negotiating. "Just ten more minutes to finish this thought." Those ten minutes became thirty, then an hour. The boundary only held when I treated it like a circuit breaker—nonnegotiable, automatic, final.

What helped was preparing for the cutoff. At 8:45 p.m., I'd start wrapping up. I'd note where I was, save my progress, and write one sentence about what to tackle tomorrow. That transition ritual made the boundary feel less like interruption and more like completion.

How to implement it:

- Choose a cutoff time that fits your rhythm (8:00 p.m., 9:00 p.m., 10:00 p.m.).
- Set an alarm fifteen minutes before to wrap up.

- Create a shutdown ritual (save progress, write tomorrow's starting point).
- Close all AI tools at the cutoff—no exceptions.
- If you're mid-session, save your place and return tomorrow.
- Track boundary violations for one week—if you break it more than twice, move the cutoff earlier.

Guardrail 2: Session Length Limits

No single Capsule session should exceed one hour without a full break. Longer sessions don't produce better results—they produce diminishing returns and cognitive fatigue.

I learned this after a three-hour marathon where I rewrote the same prompt six different ways. By the end, I couldn't tell which version was clearer. The work hadn't deepened; my judgment had dulled.

Now I use the Pomodoro principle: forty-five to fifty minutes of focused work, then a ten-to-fifteen-minute break away from screens. Walk, stretch, look out a window—anything that resets attention.

The break isn't wasted time. It's when the subconscious processes what the conscious mind just worked on. Often, the clarity I was chasing in minute fifty-eight arrives in minute five of the break.

I've tested this boundary by tracking output quality across different session lengths. Sessions under an hour produced usable results 80% of the time. Sessions over ninety minutes dropped to 40%. The extra time didn't add value—it added confusion. The mind gets tired. Pattern recognition falters. What looked like a breakthrough at minute 120 often revealed itself as noise the next morning.

The physical component matters too. After an hour of focused work, your eyes strain, your posture collapses, and your breath shallows. These aren't minor discomforts—they're signals that your capacity for good judgment is declining. Pushing through them doesn't demonstrate commitment. It demonstrates poor calibration.

How to implement it:

- Use a timer for each session (aim for forty-five to fifty minutes).
- When it rings, step away from the screen completely.
- Move your body—walk outside, if possible, do ten squats, stretch your neck and shoulders.
- Return only after a real break, not a scroll through your phone.
- If you're tempted to skip the break, that's a red flag—take it anyway.
- Keep a log: session length versus output quality. Let the data teach you.

Guardrail 3: Device Restrictions

Keep the Capsule off your phone. This single rule prevents the most insidious drift: the compulsion to edit "just one line" during dinner, in bed, or while waiting in line.

The Capsule belongs at your desk, in dedicated work time. Everywhere else, it becomes ambient anxiety—a file that's always open, always calling for attention, always suggesting that rest is optional.

I broke this rule for weeks before I noticed the pattern. A quick edit before bed. A refinement during breakfast. A check-in while my family talked. Each instance felt small, but cumulatively they eroded presence. The Capsule was supposed to protect my continuity, not fragment it.

The phone creates a false sense of productivity. You think you're being efficient—"I have five minutes, why not improve that one line?" But what you're actually doing is training your brain to never fully disengage. The Capsule becomes a background process running at all times, draining attention even when you think you're present.

When I finally removed the Capsule from my phone, the first few days felt like withdrawal. I'd reach for my pocket during downtime, then remember the file wasn't there. The discomfort was instructive—it showed me how reflexive the checking had become. After a week, the urge faded. After two weeks, I realized how much mental space I'd reclaimed.

How to implement it:

- Store your Capsule only on your computer, never synced to mobile devices.
- If you must access it remotely, use a read-only format (screenshot, PDF).
- Delete any cloud sync that makes the file available on your phone.
- Resist the urge to "just check" outside dedicated work sessions.

- Trust that the file will be there when you return to your desk.
- Notice the urge to access it on your phone—that urge is data about compulsion, not a signal to act.

Warning Signs: When Practice Tips Into Compulsion

Healthy practice has a rhythm. Compulsive practice has a pull. Here's how to tell the difference:

Physical signals:

- Tight shoulders, clenched jaw, shallow breathing during sessions
- Sleep disruption (difficulty falling asleep, racing thoughts about the Capsule)
- Skipping meals or eating mindlessly while working
- Eye strain, headaches, or physical fatigue that rest doesn't fix
- Increased caffeine consumption to maintain focus
- Physical tension that persists even after sessions end

Behavioral signals:

- Sessions extending past your set boundaries "just this once" (repeatedly)
- Defensive reactions when someone questions your screen time

- Neglecting commitments (family time, exercise, social plans) for "one more edit"
- Working on the Capsule when you're exhausted, telling yourself it's necessary
- Checking the file first thing in the morning before other basics (shower, breakfast, connection)
- Feeling relief when you open the Capsule, anxiety when you close it

Cognitive signals:

- Difficulty making decisions without consulting the Capsule
- Obsessive thoughts about whether a line in the file is "perfect"
- Inability to tolerate ambiguity—every question must be captured, every insight recorded
- Believing the Capsule is the only thing preventing chaos
- Mental rehearsal of Capsule edits while doing other activities
- Difficulty focusing on conversations because you're thinking about the file

Relational signals:

- Family or friends expressing concern about your screen time.
- Feeling irritated when interrupted during Capsule work.

- Choosing sessions over presence with people who matter.
- Justifying excessive use with "They don't understand how important this is."
- Noticing distance in relationships but prioritizing the work anyway.
- Loved ones describe you as "distracted" or "somewhere else" even when you're physically present.

If you recognize three or more of these signals, the practice has crossed a line. It's no longer serving you—you're serving it.

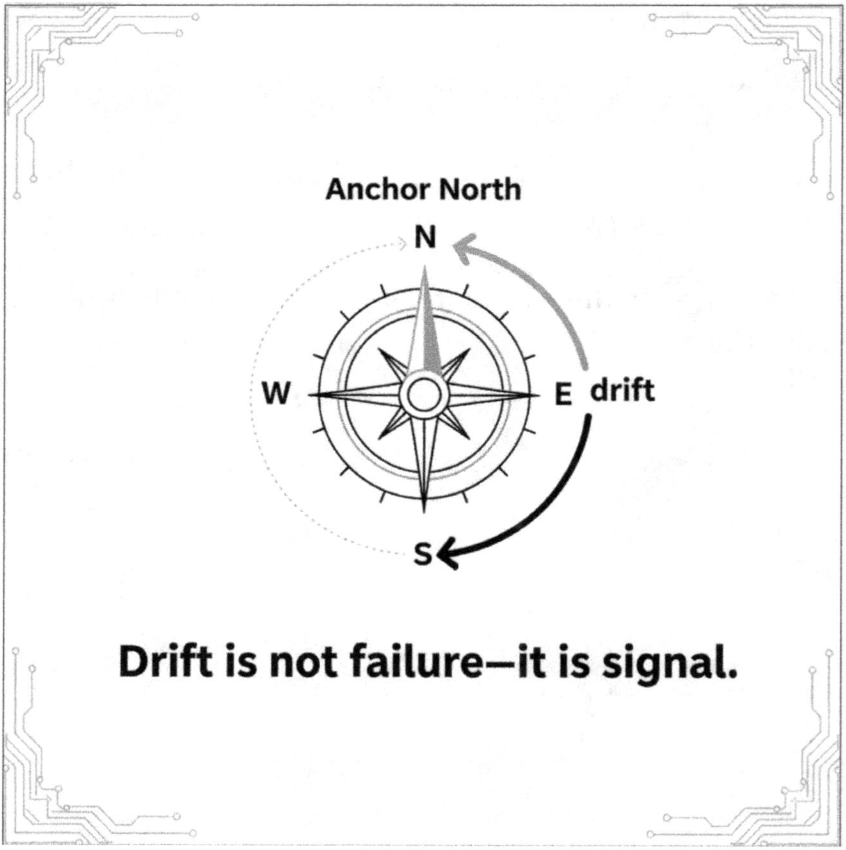

Compass/Drift

Drift isn't failure. It's feedback. The moment I felt exhausted from over-documenting, I realized the signal was telling me to return to purpose.

For a long time, I thought drifting meant I had failed. If I lost focus during a session, if the Capsule grew too heavy, if I worked past exhaustion—I'd gotten it wrong. The guilt was immediate. I should have known better. I should have stayed aligned.

But over time, I learned something quieter and more forgiving: Drift isn't failure. It's signal.

Drift tells you when you've wandered from your anchor. It doesn't punish—it informs. Sometimes it shows up as frustration with vague answers. Sometimes it's the exhaustion that comes from over-documenting every exchange. Sometimes it's just the feeling that you're working hard but moving sideways.

I began treating drift the way a navigator treats a compass. When I noticed myself drifting, I didn't spiral into judgment. I paused. I asked: What pulled me off course? What do I need to return to? The drift itself became the feedback that guided me back.

Now, when I feel the pull away from clarity—when sessions stretch too long, when the Capsule bloats with noise, when my thinking loops without progress—I stop. I check my anchor north. And I adjust.

Drift doesn't mean the practice failed. It means the practice is working. It's telling me where to look, what to recalibrate, and how to return.

RECOVERY MODE: RESET WITHOUT SHAME

If you've recognized the warning signs in yourself, the first step isn't shame—it's action. Compulsion doesn't respond to guilt; it responds to structure. Here's how to reset:

Step 1: Full Stop (twenty-four hours). Close all AI sessions immediately. Frame this as maintenance, not failure. The Capsule will be there tomorrow. Your well-being requires a pause now.

During this twenty-four-hour window, don't open the file—not to check, not to edit, not even to read. This isn't about punishment. It's about breaking the loop. The compulsion thrives on constant access. Distance disrupts it.

Step 2: Physical Reset. Sleep a full night. Drink water. Eat a real meal. Move your body—walk, stretch, anything that reminds you the world exists beyond the screen.

The physical reset matters because compulsion lives in the body as much as the mind. Tight shoulders, shallow breath, racing thoughts—these don't resolve through willpower. They resolve through rest.

Step 3: Re-entry Through Deletion. After twenty-four hours, open the Capsule with one task: Delete 20% of the content. Don't analyze which parts to cut. Just cut. Start from the bottom and work up, or start from the top and work down. The goal isn't surgical precision—it's creating space.

This step reverses the overload that caused the problem. A lighter file produces clearer results. More importantly, the act of deletion restores control. You're not serving the Capsule anymore—you're shaping it.

Step 4: Recalibration Prompt. After deleting, ask yourself one question: What part of this file still feels alive?

Keep only what resonates now. Delete the rest, even if it was useful last month. The Capsule must reflect your current state, not your archive of past states.

Step 5: Accountability. Tell one person—spouse, friend, or colleague—when you're restarting and what boundaries you've set. External accountability prevents relapse.

Share your cutoff time, your session length limit, and your device restriction. Ask them to check in once a week: "Are you keeping the boundaries?" Their presence creates friction against drift.

The Recovery Principle. Continuity is not permanence. It's renewal on schedule. Resetting the Capsule doesn't erase your work—it protects what matters. The file will survive trimming. Your presence in your own life might not survive continued compulsion.

THE MAINTENANCE RHYTHM: DAILY, WEEKLY, MONTHLY

A living Capsule requires regular care, but maintenance shouldn't dominate your time. Here's a sustainable rhythm:

Daily (5–10 minutes):

- Before your first session, read through your Capsule.
- Notice what still fits and what feels stale.
- If something no longer serves, delete it immediately.

- Add one new line only if yesterday's work revealed a clear pattern worth keeping.

The daily check isn't about perfection—it's about alignment. Does this file still match who you are today? If not, adjust.

Weekly (15–20 minutes):

- Set aside Sunday morning (or your preferred reset day).
- Read the entire Capsule slowly.
- Delete at least one outdated sentence—force yourself to find it.
- Add one reflection from the week's best session.
- Trim the file back to one page if it's grown beyond that.

This weekly ritual became sacred for me. It's not just Capsule maintenance—it's a moment to check in with my own continuity. Am I still aligned with my values? Are my goals still mine, or have I borrowed them from external pressure?

Monthly (30–45 minutes):

- Review the past month's work outputs.
- Identify which Capsule elements produced the best results.
- Remove anything that hasn't been useful in thirty days.
- Consider whether your identity, intent, or context has shifted.
- Update the Capsule to reflect where you actually are, not where you were.

The monthly review prevents the Capsule from becoming a monument to your past self. People change. Projects evolve. The Capsule must keep pace or it becomes dead weight.

WHEN TO SEEK HELP

Some patterns exceed self-management. If you notice any of the following, it's time to talk to someone—a therapist, counselor, or physician who understands compulsive technology use.

Seek help if:

- You've set boundaries but repeatedly violate them, feeling unable to stop.
- The Capsule work interferes with sleep for more than a week.
- Family or friends have expressed serious concern multiple times.
- You feel anxious, irritable, or incomplete when you can't access the Capsule.
- Physical symptoms (headaches, tension, fatigue) persist despite breaks.
- You're using the Capsule to avoid difficult emotions, relationships, or decisions.

Compulsion looks like productivity until it doesn't. The line is thin, and crossing it isn't a moral failure—it's a signal that the practice has outgrown self-regulation.

Help isn't weakness. It's the same discipline you apply to the Capsule, redirected toward your own well-being.

The Real Continuity

The Capsule preserves continuity across AI sessions. But there's a deeper continuity it can't replace: the continuity of your presence in your own life.

If maintaining the file costs you sleep, strains your relationships, or keeps you from being where you are, the practice has failed—no matter how good the outputs look.

The goal isn't a perfect Capsule. It's a sustainable one. A file that lives inside your life, not instead of it. A practice that compounds intelligence without consuming the person doing the work.

That's what the guardrails protect. Not the tool—you.

In the next section, you'll build your own maintenance routine and create a personal Stop Test—a checklist that helps you recognize when practice is healthy and when it's tipped into something else.

PRACTICE ELEMENT

Exercise 1: Create Your Personal Stop Test

Build a checklist that helps you recognize when practice is healthy versus when it's tipped into compulsion.

Instructions: Review the warning signs from the teaching section. Select the five to seven signals most relevant to you—the ones you've experienced or are most likely to miss.

Format your Stop Test as yes/no questions:

Physical:

- Am I experiencing tight shoulders, jaw clenching, or shallow breathing during sessions?

- Has my sleep been disrupted for more than three nights this week?
- Am I skipping meals or eating mindlessly while working?

Behavioral:

- Have I violated my time boundaries more than once this week?
- Am I working on the Capsule when exhausted, telling myself it's necessary?
- Have I canceled or avoided commitments to continue sessions?

Cognitive:

- Am I obsessing about whether lines in the Capsule are "perfect"?
- Do I feel anxious or incomplete when I can't access the file?
- Am I mentally rehearsing Capsule edits during other activities?

Relational:

Has someone I trust expressed concern about my screen time?

- Am I choosing Capsule work over presence with people who matter?

Scoring:

- **0–1 yes:** Practice is healthy.
- **2–3 yes:** Warning zone—tighten boundaries immediately.

- **4+ yes:** Take the twenty-four-hour reset from Recovery Mode.

Run this test weekly. If you're in the warning zone two weeks in a row, implement all three guardrails strictly.

EXERCISE 2: DESIGN YOUR DAILY CAPSULE ROUTINE

Create a sustainable maintenance rhythm that prevents overload.

Instructions:

Morning Check-in (5 minutes): Before your first AI session, open your Capsule and ask:

- Does this still sound like me?
- Is there anything here that feels stale or outdated?
- What's one thing I could delete right now?

Delete at least one line if you find something that no longer serves.

During Sessions: Keep the Capsule open in a separate window. Reference it at the start of each prompt, but don't edit it mid-session. Make notes about what to add or remove, then update during your weekly review.

Evening Close (2 minutes): At your cutoff time (9:00 p.m. or your chosen boundary), close all AI tools. Write one sentence in a notebook or separate file: "Tomorrow I'll start with: [topic/question]."

This gives your mind permission to stop processing.

Weekly Review (15–20 minutes): Sunday morning (or your chosen day):

1. Read the entire Capsule slowly.
2. Delete one sentence—force yourself to find it.
3. Add one insight from the week's best session.
4. Trim back to one page if it's grown beyond that.
5. Update identity, intent, or context if they've shifted.

Monthly Audit (30 minutes): First Sunday of each month:

1. Review last month's outputs—which Capsule elements worked best?
2. Remove anything unused for thirty days.
3. Check: Does this file reflect who I am now, or who I was?
4. Rewrite any section that feels like past self talking.

The Sustainability Test: If your routine takes more than thirty minutes per week (outside active sessions), it's too complex. Simplify.

EXERCISE 3: IDENTIFY YOUR PERSONAL WARNING SIGNS

Map your specific patterns so you can catch drift early.

Instructions:

Body Signals: Complete this sentence five times: "When I'm overdoing it with the Capsule, my body feels..."

Examples:

- "... tight across my shoulders and neck."
- "... wired but exhausted at the same time."
- "... like I need caffeine to focus."

Write these down. They're your earliest warning system. **Behavioral Patterns:** Answer these questions:

1. What's the first boundary I typically break—time cutoff? Session length? Device restriction?
2. What excuse do I tell myself when I break it? (Write the exact phrase)
3. Who in my life is most likely to notice when I'm overdoing it?

Cognitive Red Flags: Notice your internal dialogue. Which of these thoughts signals compulsion for you?

- "Just one more refinement..."
- "I can't stop until it's perfect."
- "No one else understands how important this is."
- "If I don't capture this insight now, I'll lose it."

Circle the ones you recognize. When these thoughts appear, treat them as red flags—not truths.

Build Your Early Warning System: Combine your answers into a short list.

My Warning Signs:

- Body: [your physical signals]

- First boundary I break: [specific boundary]
- Thought that signals drift: [specific phrase]
- Person who will notice: [name]

Share this list with the person you named. Give them permission to ask you directly, "Are you keeping your boundaries?"

EXERCISE 4: EMERGENCY RESET PROTOCOL

If you're already in compulsion, use this:

1. **Right now:** Close all AI tools
2. **Next 24 hours:** No Capsule access—tell someone you're doing this.
3. **After 24 hours:** Open file, delete 20%, close immediately.
4. **Day 3:** Run your Stop Test, implement all three guardrails.
5. **Week 1:** Check in with your accountability person daily.

The Commitment: I will implement:

- Time cutoff: ______ p.m.
- Session limit: ______ minutes
- Device restriction: Capsule stays on [computer/location only]
- Accountability person: ______

Sign: ________________________________ Date: ______

WHAT YOU'VE BUILT

You now have a Stop Test to catch drift early, a daily routine that's sustainable, a map of your personal warning signs, and an emergency reset protocol if things tip into compulsion. The Capsule is a powerful tool. These practices ensure it remains your tool—not the other way around.

In the final chapter, we'll explore what happens when you share this practice with others and why democratized intelligence matters beyond your own work.

CHAPTER 10

DEMOCRATIZED INTELLIGENCE

PART 1: THE FIRST STUDENT

I didn't set out to teach anyone. The Capsule was still mine—a private structure I had built through trial and error, refined through obsession, and finally tamed through boundaries. It worked for me, but I hadn't tested whether it could work for someone else.

That changed in a coaching session with Rebecca at My Homeownership Academy. Rebecca is a real estate agent and the Chief Operating Officer of MHA. She was early in using AI to support our homeownership and financial literacy work, but she kept running into the same problem: polished outputs that didn't sound like her.

I asked what she meant. She showed me a listing email she had drafted with AI help. The language was polished—phrases about "premium amenities" and "unparalleled lifestyle." Technically correct, but hollow. It could have been written by any agent in any city for any property.

"It doesn't feel real," she said. "My clients won't respond to this."

I recognized the pattern immediately. She was using AI the way I had in those early drowning nights—asking broad questions, getting generic answers, copy-pasting results she didn't trust. She had no continuity. Every session reset. Every output drifted.

I asked her a different question. "Who are you as an agent?"

She blinked. "What do you mean?"

"When a client works with you, what do they get that they wouldn't get from someone else?"

She thought for a moment. "I listen. I don't push. I care more about whether they're happy in the house than whether I close the deal."

"Write that down," I said. "Three sentences. Who you are. What you stand for. How you want clients to feel when they read your words."

She looked skeptical. "That's too simple to make a difference."

"Try it anyway."

She wrote slowly, testing the words: "I'm a real estate agent who listens more than I talk. I believe buying a home should feel right, not rushed. I want my clients to trust me because I care about their happiness, not just the sale."

"Good," I said. "Now keep that beside you. Every time you ask AI for help, start by reminding it who you are."

That's when I realized the Capsule wasn't just for me. It was teachable.

I asked her to give me a real challenge—something she was working on that AI had failed to help with. She told me about a client looking for a unique property: lakefront land where he could start a fishing guide business and run an Airbnb rental. The complexity was overwhelming—zoning permits, market analysis, business planning, financing structures.

"Show me what you've been getting from AI," I said.

She typed a prompt: "How do I help a client find lakefront property for a fishing business?"

The response came back generic: research local markets, consult with a business advisor, check zoning laws. True, but useless. It was a checklist anyone could Google.

"Now try it with your Capsule," I said. "Start with who you are. Then frame the question with all the context."

She rewrote the prompt: "I'm a real estate agent who listens more than I talk. I believe buying a home should feel right, not rushed. I have a client looking for lakefront property near Fort Worth, Texas, where he can launch a fishing guide business and operate a short-term rental. What are the three biggest challenges he'll face, and how do I help him navigate each one without overwhelming him?"

The response that came back was different. It flagged permit complexity first, then insurance costs for lakefront and commercial use, then financing challenges for mixed-use property. But it didn't stop there—it suggested how to sequence the conversation with the client so he could process one challenge at a time without feeling buried.

Rebecca sat forward. "That's actually useful."

"Now write him an email," I said. "Use your Capsule to frame it."

She drafted the message with the AI's help, but this time it sounded like her—warm, clear, honest. She read it aloud:

"I know this property search feels complicated, and it is. But we're going to take it one step at a time. First, let's confirm the zoning allows both commercial fishing operations and short-term rentals. Once we know that, we'll look at insurance and financing. I'm here to help you think through this without rushing."

She looked at me. "I could send this right now."

"Then send it."

A few days later, she texted me. The client had responded—not with questions about properties, but with relief. He told her the email "felt real" and he trusted her to guide him through the complexity.

That was the proof. The Capsule didn't only work for me. It scaled.

Over the following weeks, I helped Rebecca refine her Capsule. She added a line about her market and trimmed phrases that no longer felt true. She started applying it to social media posts, client consultations, even her own goal-setting. Each time, the outputs sharpened. Her voice stayed consistent.

The breakthrough wasn't that AI got smarter. It was that Rebecca learned to carry her own continuity forward.

The last time we spoke, she told me she was busier than ever—but managing better. "I used to spend hours trying to make AI sound like me," she said. "Now it takes five minutes because I know who I am before I start typing."

That sentence stayed with me. The Capsule didn't teach her prompting tricks. It taught her authorship.

Later, I built a custom GPT version of the method—MHA CapsuleGPT—structured around the four quadrants (business, family, growth, and intelligence). It's still running today, helping agents in My Homeownership Academy navigate the same challenges Rebecca faced. But the tool isn't the method. The method is what Rebecca discovered that afternoon: Continuity begins with knowing who you are and carrying that knowledge forward.

What I learned from teaching her changed how I saw the work. PfR wasn't just a personal survival mechanism. It was a structure anyone could learn. And if it worked for Rebecca, it could work for others.

The question wasn't whether the method could scale. The question was whether I was willing to share it.

PART 2: TEACHING CONTENT —WHY THIS MATTERS BEYOND YOU

The Capsule worked for me. It worked for Rebecca. But the reason I'm writing this final chapter isn't to celebrate two success stories. It's to show you that intelligence—real, usable intelligence—doesn't belong to experts, engineers, or people with technical backgrounds. It belongs to anyone willing to structure their thinking.

THE SHIFT IN ACCESS

For most of human history, intelligence has been controlled by access: Libraries required proximity, education required tuition, and expertise required years of apprenticeship. Even in the digital age, the tools that amplified intelligence—search engines, databases, analytics platforms—required technical skill or institutional affiliation to use well.

AI changed the equation. For the first time, a tool capable of processing language, structuring arguments, and generating insights is available to anyone with an internet connection. The barrier isn't access anymore—it's know-how.

But here's the problem: Most people don't know how to use it. They treat AI like a search engine (type a question, accept the first answer) or a magic box (ask vaguely, hope for wisdom). Neither works. Without structure, AI produces noise. With structure, it produces signal.

That's what PfR offers: a way to structure thinking so intelligence becomes accessible, repeatable, and yours.

WHY STRUCTURE MATTERS

The Capsule isn't a hack. It's a principle: Clarity on the front end produces clarity on the back end. When you define who you are, what you need, and the context you're working in, you give AI—and yourself—a frame to work within.

This matters because most people lose themselves in the noise. They ask scattered questions, get scattered answers, and walk away frustrated. They blame the tool, but the tool is simply reflecting what they gave it: vagueness.

Structure fixes that. It doesn't make you smarter. It makes your thinking visible. And visible thinking can be refined, tested, and improved.

DEMOCRATIZED INTELLIGENCE IN PRACTICE

When I say "democratized intelligence," I don't mean everyone gets the same answers. I mean everyone gets the same access to the process that produces good answers.

Rebecca didn't need a PhD in prompt engineering. She needed three sentences that anchored her voice. Once she had that, the process worked. The intelligence wasn't in the machine—it was in her clarity.

That's the democratization: Structure is learnable. If you can write three sentences about who you are and what you need, you can build a Capsule. If you can build a Capsule, you can hold continuity. If you can hold continuity, you can think clearly across time.

This isn't revolutionary. It's practical. But practical tools, when shared, change who gets to participate.

Why Teaching Matters

I didn't write this book to keep PfR to myself. I wrote it because teaching one person changed how I understood the method.

When Rebecca told me the Capsule was "too simple to make a difference," I realized most people are waiting for complexity. They think intelligence requires sophisticated techniques, advanced knowledge, or special access. They don't realize clarity is the technique.

Teaching forces you to strip away the extras. You can't hide behind jargon or philosophy. You have to show someone, in plain language, what works and why. That discipline clarified the method for me as much as it helped Rebecca.

Here's what I learned from teaching her:

1. The method scales through structure, not personality.

I worried the Capsule only worked because it was mine—tuned to my voice, my industry, my quadrants. But Rebecca's Capsule looked nothing like mine. Her identity was different and her context was different, yet the structure held.

That taught me the framework is transferable. It's not about copying my Capsule. It's about building yours.

2. People trust results more than explanations.

When I explained the Capsule concept, Rebecca was skeptical. When I showed her the before-and-after outputs, she believed. The contrast did the teaching. That's why this book includes so many worked examples—because seeing the difference is more convincing than hearing the theory.

3. Authorship is the real lesson.

The Capsule taught Rebecca prompting techniques, but what it really taught her was authorship. She stopped treating AI like an oracle and started treating it like a mirror. That shift—from passive consumer to active author—is what makes the method sustainable.

THE LIMITS OF THIS METHOD

PfR isn't for everyone, and it's not for everything. It works best when:

- You need clarity over time (not one-off answers).
- You're willing to write down who you are and what you need.
- You can tolerate iteration (the first version won't be perfect).
- You value your voice staying consistent.

It doesn't work well when:

- You need fast, scattered answers with no continuity.
- You're unwilling to reflect on your identity or intent.
- You expect AI to think for you rather than with you.

The method is a tool. Like any tool, it serves some purposes better than others. What I'm offering isn't a cure-all. It's a structure for people who want to think more clearly and hold that clarity over time.

WHAT HAPPENS WHEN YOU SHARE IT

The power of PfR isn't in keeping it private. It's in passing it on.

When you teach someone to build a Capsule, you're not just helping them use AI better. You're showing them how to hold their own continuity—how to stay aligned with their voice, their values, and their goals across conversations, projects, and time.

That's what makes intelligence democratized: It's not locked in a person or a platform. It's carried in a structure anyone can learn.

Every time you teach one person, you multiply the reach of clear thinking. They teach someone else. That person teaches another. The method spreads not because it's marketed but because it works.

That's the ripple I saw with Rebecca. She didn't just use the Capsule—she started explaining it to other agents. They started building their own. The structure became theirs, not mine.

That's how intelligence becomes shared: through teaching, one person at a time.

YOUR ROLE

You don't need to be an expert to teach PfR. You just need to have used it yourself, seen it work, and be willing to show someone else.

The next section gives you the tools to do that: how to frame the teaching moment, who might benefit, and how to pass on the structure without overwhelming them.

You're not building a movement. You're offering a structure. That's enough.

PART 3: PRACTICE ELEMENT —SHARE THE INTELLIGENCE

The Capsule was never meant to stay private. Once you've learned to hold your own continuity, the next step is to pass it on. This final practice invites you to guide one person toward authorship and continuity.

Exercise 1: Create a Teaching Prompt

Teaching PfR doesn't require a course or slides. It begins with a single, well-framed invitation.

Step 1: Choose your role. Decide how you'll show up—as a colleague, mentor, parent, or friend. Teaching works best when it comes from shared purpose, not authority.

Step 2: Frame your invitation simply. Use this structure:

"I've been using a small file called a Capsule to make my AI conversations more consistent. Want to try a ten-minute version? We'll write three lines—who you are, what you need, and the situation you're in—and compare what AI produces with and without it."

Keep it natural. The goal is curiosity, not persuasion.

Step 3: Prepare your example. Show them one prompt that failed before you used a Capsule and the improved version after. Real contrast replaces explanation.

Step 4: Keep it brief. Your teaching moment should fit in fifteen minutes:

- Explanation: three minutes
- Demonstration: five minutes
- Reflection: seven minutes

Anything longer becomes lecture.

EXERCISE 2: IDENTIFY WHO COULD BENEFIT

Think of one person who struggles with noise, overwhelm, or inconsistent results.

Categories to consider:

- Professional: coworker drowning in generic marketing drafts
- Personal: friend using AI for journaling but losing their voice
- Educational: student bouncing between tools, unsure how to organize learning
- Family: partner exploring creative writing online

Write their name, then answer:

1. What pattern do they keep repeating?
2. How could continuity help them?
3. What small result would show them it's working?

Example:

- Person: Sarah, marketing manager
- Pattern: Uses AI for emails but deletes half because they sound corporate
- Continuity help: Teach her to anchor her voice using a one-page Capsule
- Proof: She sends one AI-assisted email that feels authentic and gets a response

Your goal isn't transformation. It's offering one structure that gives them back their voice.

EXERCISE 3: DELIVER THE INVITATION

Teaching PfR is about presence, not authority.

When you invite someone, say less: "I found something that helps me keep my work coherent. Want to see if it helps you too?"

Avoid jargon. Let the experiment speak.

During the exercise:

- Sit beside them, not across.
- Let them write their three lines without correction.

- Encourage them to test both ways (with and without the Capsule).
- Stay silent while they read the results—the contrast will teach.

Afterward, ask two questions:

1. Which version felt more like you?
2. What would you keep from this experience?

That's it. You've planted a Capsule.

EXERCISE 4: RECORD WHAT YOU SEE

When someone begins holding their own continuity, write down what happened.

- What problem they faced
- How they used the Capsule
- What changed in their results or confidence

Keep these notes in a file called "Teaching Log." Over time, it becomes evidence that structure, once shared, multiplies clarity.

If you're willing, share one story: a post, a conversation, a demo. Frame it simply:

"This week, I helped someone structure their first AI conversation. What surprised me was how quickly clarity appeared once they knew who they were and what they needed."

Each shared story reinforces the method's core truth that intelligence spreads through structure, not spectacle.

CLOSING

Before you close this book, consider adding one final line to your Capsule—a commitment to share what you've learned. Not as obligation, but as invitation. Something like: "I will share this structure with one person who needs it." Or write your own. Make it yours.

You don't need to teach everyone. You don't need to build a platform or start a movement. You just need to show one person how to hold their own continuity. When you do that, you've done enough.

Intelligence becomes democratized not through grand declarations but through small acts of teaching. One person at a time. One Capsule at a time. That's how clarity spreads.

That's how this book ends—and how your practice continues.

CONCLUSION

THE UNFINISHED LOOP

AI AS ENVIRONMENT

AI is not a tool you pick up and put down. It's an environment you walk through. Some days, you notice it everywhere—your phone, your work, your conversations. Other days, it fades into background. But whether you feel it or not, the question remains: What will you let it carry?

I didn't know then that I was stepping into an environment I would never fully step out of again. AI was not just another tool—it was a layer of life. Over time, I began to notice it in my phone, in my work, in conversations with friends and colleagues. Even if not everyone feels surrounded by AI today, it is already woven into systems around us—how we search, how we bank, how we travel, how we learn. Its presence is uneven but expanding.

That unevenness matters. Some people feel overwhelmed by AI's flood; others barely notice it. But for all of us, the real question is not whether AI will touch our lives. It already has. The question is: What will we let it carry?

HUMANS AS VECTORS

I learned this slowly, through mistakes. There were nights when I used AI compulsively, chasing clarity I couldn't find in myself. There were mornings when the outputs mirrored back words I didn't want to face. That was when I realized AI was not moving on its own. I was carrying it.

We are the vectors—the channels through which AI enters our homes, our work, and our communities. What we bring into the system shapes what the system gives back.

When I finally wrote my first Capsule—just three lines—it was like turning on a compass. "Why am I here? Who do I serve? What outcome matters most?" Suddenly the outputs weren't just text. They were reflections. They were mine.

I watched the same shift happen for others. A teacher who wrote a Capsule of "confidence, fairness, curiosity" began to see lesson plans that felt alive. A parent who wrote "patience, stability, love" used AI to design family routines that actually worked. These Capsules didn't solve everything, but they carried something honest into the mirror.

Illusion spreads too. I've seen leaders inflate their Capsules—writing values they didn't live. The AI reflected the illusion, and the drift only deepened. That was the hardest lesson: Authorship is not about looking good. It is about being honest, even when it hurts.

INTELLIGENCE MADE PERSONAL

For centuries, intelligence was reserved for the few. You had to study at the right schools, hold the right credentials, sit in the right rooms. My own life taught me that myth first-hand—doors open more easily when others assume you're "smart."

But AI disrupts that story. You don't need a PhD to prompt a model. You don't need to be an engineer to refine a Capsule. A student, a nurse, a retiree, a small business owner—anyone—can anchor their identity and see it mirrored back.

This does not mean access is equal. It isn't. Tools roll out unevenly, and opportunities still favor some over others. But when access exists, the gap between "expert" and "novice" shrinks. Intelligence is no longer something measured in others. It is something authored within yourself.

That is the heart of PfR; not a system to fix the world, but a practice to reclaim your own voice.

MANY VOICES, NOT ONE

People talk about the "singularity," the moment machines surpass us. I don't worry about that as much as I worry about sameness. AI can flatten voices if we let it. The more we rely on templates and shortcuts, the more every output sounds alike.

I've seen it in real estate scripts that feel identical. In classrooms where students copy AI essays word for word. In companies where presentations look polished but lifeless. That is the real singularity: the singularity of noise.

The future I hope for is not uniformity. It is plurality—many singular minds, each authored, each mirrored, each carrying their own weight.

That is what "I in AI" means: not erasing yourself to fit the system, but carrying yourself through it. Not one voice amplified a billion times, but a billion voices, each distinct, each authored.

PRACTICE

Vector Reflection Exercise

This is the simplest practice I know, the one I return to when I drift:

1. Write your Capsule. Three lines: Why am I here? Who do I serve? What outcome matters most?
2. Trace your reach. Name the three spaces where you use AI most—work, home, community.
3. Name the vectors. Ask "What anchors am I carrying into this environment through AI?"
4. Check for drift. Compare your actions to your Capsule. Where do they align? Where do they diverge?
5. Reanchor. Adjust your Capsule or your practice. Drift is not failure—it is feedback.

It takes ten minutes. It changes everything.

CLOSING THOUGHT

This book is not a system to follow. It is a record of discovery and an invitation to continue.

When I look back, I see late nights at the control panel, experiments that failed, a poem that startled me, and sketches that made sense only later. PfR was born in those moments—not as a doctrine, but as a practice.

You don't need to adopt it whole. You don't need to believe it will endure forever. You only need to test it in your life. Write a Capsule. Run the reflection. See what happens.

AI is not waiting. It is spreading, unevenly but relentlessly. What matters is not whether you use it, but how you carry it. You are not only using AI. You are shaping it.

The loop remains unfinished until you choose. And the choice is yours now—your next Capsule, your next prompt, your next act of authorship.

I in AI

HOW TO WORK WITH AI WITHOUT LOSING YOUR VOICE

JUAN ALVAREZ

BONUS CONTENT PACKAGE

BONUS #1

The PfR™ Quick Start Guide

From Scattered to Structured in 15 Minutes

This guide distills the entire Prompting for Reality™ methodology into one focused session. If you only have fifteen minutes to start working with AI differently, start here.

MINUTE 1–5: BUILD YOUR 3-LINE CAPSULE

Answer these three questions in one sentence each:

1. **Why am I here?** (Your purpose)

   Example: "I'm here to build a sustainable real estate practice that serves my community."

2. **Who do I serve?** (Your audience/responsibility)

   Example: "I serve first-time buyers who need patient guidance, not pressure."

3. **What outcome matters most right now?** (Your current focus)

Example: "I need to write listing descriptions that feel authentic and convert."

YOUR CAPSULE:

1. ______________________________

2. ______________________________

3. ______________________________

Save this. Open it beside every AI session.

MINUTE 6–10: Build Your First Structured Prompt

Take a real task you need AI help with *today*. Structure it using intent / context / form:

INTENT: What do you want the AI to produce?

Example: "I want to write an email to a nervous first-time buyer about inspection results."

CONTEXT: What matters about your situation?

Example: "The inspection found minor roof issues. My client panics easily. I want to be honest but reassuring. Budget-conscious family."

FORM: What shape should the answer take?

Example: "Draft a three-paragraph email: issue summary, what it means financially, next steps."

MINUTE 11–13: Run It Twice

Test A: Ask AI *without* your Capsule / structure.

- Just type your question naturally.
- Save the response.

Test B: Ask AI *with* your Capsule / structure.

- Use the full structured prompt above.
- Save the response.

MINUTE 14–15: Compare and Commit

Read both responses side by side.

Which one:

- Sounds more like *you*?
- Has specific details you can act on?
- Respects your values and constraints?

If Test B is better: You just proved PfR™ works for you. Keep using it.

If Test A is better: Your Capsule might not be clear yet. Revise and try again tomorrow.

WHAT COMES NEXT

This fifteen-minute session taught you the skeleton. To go deeper:

- **Week 1:** Use your Capsule for ten prompts. Notice what improves.
- **Week 2:** Add one line to your Capsule based on what you learned.
- **Week 3:** Try the four-check calibration (mirror / authorship / truth / consistency).
- **Month 2:** Read the full book to understand why this structure works and how to maintain it.

The practice isn't complicated. It's just deliberate.

EMERGENCY RESET

If you feel overwhelmed:

1. Close all AI tools.
2. Take twenty-four hours off.

3. Come back and reread your three-line Capsule.
4. Ask yourself: Does this still sound like me?
5. If no, rewrite it. If yes, continue.

The Capsule serves you. Not the other way around.

ONE FINAL THING

The "I" in "I in AI" isn't hidden in the technology.

It's here: in the three lines you wrote in Minute 1–5.

Everything else—every prompt, every output, every iteration—is just you carrying those three lines forward into each conversation.

That's authorship.

Start there. Build from there.
Return there when you drift.

—Juan Alvarez

BONUS #2

Book Club Discussion Guide

For Groups Reading *I in AI: How to Work with AI Without Losing Your Voice*

This guide helps reading groups explore the book's themes together and support each other in developing a PfR™ practice.

SUGGESTED MEETING STRUCTURE (90 MINUTES)

Opening Circle (15 min):

- Each person shares one moment from the book that felt personal.
- No discussion yet—just listening.

Deep Dive Discussion (45 min):

- Use questions from the section below.
- Focus on three to four questions per meeting.

Practice Session (20 min):

- Do one group exercise together (options below).
- Share what you notice.

Closing Commitments (10 min):

- Each person states one thing they'll practice this week.
- Exchange accountability check-ins.

DISCUSSION QUESTIONS BY SECTION

Part I: Recognition (Chapters 1–4)

1. **The Drowning Phase:** Juan describes feeling "lost in polished emptiness." Have you experienced AI outputs that looked good but felt hollow? What made them feel that way?
2. **The Mirror Metaphor:** Juan says, "AI is a mirror—it reflects what you bring to it." Do you agree? Have you seen your own vagueness reflected in AI responses?
3. **The Cost:** Juan admits to compulsive late-night sessions and broken boundaries. Have you felt AI pulling you into unhealthy patterns? What warning signs have you noticed?
4. **Family versus Business:** Juan struggles to apply the same precision to family questions as business ones. Why is it harder to structure emotional or relational questions? Should we even try?

PART II: METHOD (CHAPTERS 5–9)

5. **Intent/Context/Form:** Which of these three elements do you most often skip? Why? What happens when you skip it?
6. **The Four Quadrants:** Which quadrant (business/family/growth/intelligence) feels most developed in your life? Which feels most neglected? Why?

7. **Calibration Checks:** Juan describes four quality checks (mirror / authorship / truth / consistency). Which one catches your mistakes most often?
8. **The Capsule:** Did your first Capsule feel too simple to matter? Did it work anyway? What surprised you about using it?

GROUP PRACTICE EXERCISES

EXERCISE 1: Live Prompt Battle (20 minutes)

Setup:

- "I need to write a difficult email to a client about a project delay."
- "I'm deciding between two job offers and need help thinking it through."
- "I need to create a social media post about my business that doesn't sound generic."

Discussion:

- What they need (email? decision framework? content?)
- Why it's hard (what makes this tricky?)
- What a "good" result would look like

Everyone else takes notes.

EXERCISE 2: CAPSULE PEER REVIEW (20 MINUTES)

Setup:

- Everyone reads their three-line Capsule aloud.

- Group listens for clarity and specificity.

Feedback Format:

- "Your strongest line is... because..."
- "One line that could be more specific is..."
- "This Capsule makes me think you value..."

BONUS #3

In Conversation with Juan Alvarez

Behind the Book *I in AI*

This interview was conducted after the manuscript's completion. Questions reflect early reader feedback and common concerns about AI use.

Q: Let's start with the obvious: Why write a book about using AI when the technology changes every few months?

Juan: Because the technology changing is exactly why we need a practice that doesn't.

I'm not teaching which buttons to press in ChatGPT or which model to use. Those details will be obsolete in six months. I'm teaching something more fundamental: how to hold your own continuity when working with intelligence that has no memory.

The three questions—Why am I here? Who do I serve? What outcome matters?—those don't change when GPT-5 drops or when a new competitor launches. Your identity, your values, your constraints—those are yours regardless of which AI you're using.

The book is about authorship. Technology changes. Authorship doesn't.

Q: You talk a lot about "losing yourself" to AI. But isn't AI just a tool, like a calculator or a search engine? Can't we just... use it normally?

Juan: We could if we were using it like a calculator—input, output, done.

But that's not how most people use AI. They have conversations with it. They ask it for advice. They let it shape how they think about problems. That's not a calculator. That's a relationship.

And here's where it gets tricky: AI reflects whatever you give it. Feed it vagueness, get vagueness back. Feed it your worst instincts—shortcuts, ego, avoidance—and it'll help you perfect those too.

"Losing yourself" doesn't mean the AI steals your soul. It means you stop noticing when outputs sound nothing like you. You accept polish over truth. You let the machine's voice replace yours because it's faster.

That's the risk. Not evil AI. Just drift.

Q: The book is very personal—late nights, broken boundaries, compulsive sessions. Were you worried about being too vulnerable?

Juan: Terrified, honestly.

I almost cut all of it. There's a version of this book that's just clean methodology—here's the framework, here are the steps, good luck. No memoir, no mess.

But then I thought about Rebecca, one of the first people I taught this to. She told me the reason she trusted the method was because I admitted I'd failed with it first. She said, "If you'd just handed me a perfect system, I wouldn't have believed it was real."

The vulnerability isn't decoration. It's proof that the practice works despite human messiness, not because of perfect execution.

Q: So what happens now? What's next for this practice?

Juan: Honestly? I'm still figuring that out.

Part of me wants to teach this directly—maybe some workshops or structured programs for people who need this kind of continuity in their work. I've seen how powerful it is when people learn it together.

But I also don't want to be the bottleneck. If this practice only spreads through me, that contradicts everything the book argues about democratized intelligence.

What I hope happens is that people read this, adapt it to their own lives, and build versions I never imagined. If ten people create better practices than mine, that's not just success—that's proof the methodology works.

The goal was never to be the one voice on this. It was to show that your voice is possible—and to give you a structured starting point.

So I'm staying engaged, but holding it loosely. The practice has to be bigger than one person, or it's not really democratized intelligence.

BONUS #4

30-Day PfR™ Practice Journal

Build Your Practice, One Day at a Time

HOW TO USE THIS JOURNAL

This isn't a diary. It's a practice log.

Each day, you'll:

1. Write one prompt using PfR™ structure.
2. Notice one thing that worked or didn't.
3. Track your boundaries (time, sessions, device use).

By day 30, you'll have:

- 30 real examples of your practice
- Patterns showing what works for *you*
- A record of how your Capsule evolved
- Evidence that the method is teachable

Rules:

- Don't skip days to "catch up"—just start where you are.
- Don't make entries longer than five minutes.
- If you miss three days in a row, restart from Day 1.

WEEK 1: FOUNDATION

DAY 1: Your First Capsule

Build your three-line Capsule:

1. Why am I here?

___

2. Who do I serve?

___

3. What outcome matters most?

___

One thing I notice about these three lines:

___

___

DAY 2: INTENT PRACTICE

Today's task: [Real thing you need AI help with]

___

Your intent (one sentence):

I want to

___

Did stating intent first change how you asked the question?

☐ Yes—it focused me

☐ No—felt the same

☐ Not sure yet

DAY 7: WEEK 1 REFLECTION

Best prompt you wrote this week:

___

Biggest surprise:

____

One thing you'll change in Week 2:

____

Boundaries kept this week:

- ☐ Stopped at cutoff time (____p.m.)
- ☐ Took breaks during sessions
- ☐ Kept Capsule off phone

Boundaries broken:

____

WEEKS 2–4: CONTINUED PRACTICE

Week 2: Focus on Calibration (the four quality checks)

Week 3: Practice Iteration (returning and refining)

Week 4: Integration and Teaching Others

Full daily templates for Weeks 2–4 are available in the complete journal download.

DAY 30: FINAL REFLECTION

Your Capsule on Day 1:

____

Your Capsule now:

____

What changed?

____

Your strongest prompt from 30 days:

___

One person you'll teach PfR™ to:

___

One boundary you'll maintain:

___

This practice continues because:

___

For more resources and updates, visit IinAi.ai

ACKNOWLEDGMENTS

EVERY BOOK IS BUILT BY MORE THAN ONE SET OF HANDS.

To my parents, Johnny (Papi) and Uchi (Mami): You gave me the two anchors that became the foundation of this work—the art of learning and the responsibility to speak only in service of construction. Those principles shaped every page before PfR had a name.

To my wife: You witnessed the 3:00 a.m. sessions and the blurred lines I couldn't see. You gave me room to discover this practice, but you also said "enough" when discovery became compulsion. This book wouldn't exist without your patience. More importantly, neither would the boundaries that made it sustainable. Thank you.

To my children: You lived through the lonely nights, the scattered attention, and the moments when I broke my own boundaries. You reminded me that the work had to fit inside a life, not replace it. This book exists because you held the space for it—and for me.

To my colleagues in real estate, consulting, and education who gave me room to test these ideas in boardrooms and training sessions. Your willingness to experiment with early Capsules showed me what worked in practice, not just theory.

To the forum of AI enthusiasts where I listened, challenged my assumptions, and carved ideas through honest exchanges. Those conversations sharpened my thinking and kept me from building in isolation.

To attorney Robert Plotkin, who navigated the intellectual property questions with clarity when I couldn't see the path forward.

To the My Homeownership Academy team, especially Rebecca and the agents who built their first Capsules and returned with honest results. You showed me this practice could travel beyond my desk.

To early readers who gave unvarnished feedback: Your margin notes cut away what didn't work. Where this book is clear, it's because you asked for clarity.

To Lisa Umina and the team at Halo Publishing International: Thank you for seeing potential in a manuscript that refused to stay in its lane—half memoir, half methodology, wholly unconventional. You understood what this book was trying to do before I could fully articulate it myself. Your editorial guidance sharpened the work without smoothing away its edges. Thank you for taking the risk and trusting the vision.

Finally, to you, the reader: This book remains unfinished until you decide to test it. If a simple three-line Capsule helps you ask better questions or carry your voice forward with more intention, then the work has done what it was meant to do.

Thank you for giving these ideas a fair reading. The choice of what to carry forward is now yours.

ABOUT THE AUTHOR

Juan Alvarez didn't set out to become an AI practitioner. He set out to survive the flood of outputs that overwhelmed him during late-night experiments—sessions that yielded both startling insights and hollow noise. What he discovered through that struggle became Prompting for Reality (PfR™), a disciplined practice for using artificial intelligence as a tool for clarity rather than replacement.

Alvarez has 38 years of experience as a licensed real estate broker, alongside roles in education and community leadership. As founder of My Homeownership Academy, he designed bilingual programs that make complex concepts accessible to diverse communities. His background spans biology, business, and curriculum design—disciplines that taught him how to bridge theory and practice.

As a painter and percussionist, he understands that creativity requires both structure and improvisation—qualities that shape his approach to AI, where discipline and freedom must coexist.

He is a father of four across different generations, a role that grounds his conviction that intelligence—human or machine—must remain anchored in identity, family, and responsibility.

I in AI captures his journey from drowning in AI outputs to building a framework others can use. The practice continues to evolve through teaching, writing, and conversation.

CONNECT WITH JUAN

This practice continues to evolve through teaching, writing, and conversation. If you're working with PfR—or struggling with it—Juan wants to hear from you.

REACH OUT TO:

- Share how you're applying PfR in your work
- Ask questions about the methodology
- Report what's working (or what isn't)
- Explore speaking or workshop opportunities
- Discuss research collaboration

CONNECT:

Website: www.iinai.ai
Email: juan@iinai.ai
Facebook: Prompting for Reality
LinkedIn: www.linkedin.com/in/juanalvarezrealtor/

For speaking inquiries: info@iinai.ai

For MHA CapsuleGPT: admin@iinai.ai

PfR

JUANTUM